Looking Unto Him

By Frank E. Gaebelein

Looking Unto Him

A MESSAGE FOR EACH DAY

by
FRANK E. GAEBELEIN
Headmaster, The Stony Brook School

ZONDERVAN PUBLISHING HOUSE
GRAND RAPIDS, MICHIGAN

PREFACE

In November, 1934, the author began writing daily comments upon Scripture texts. These comments, under the title of "A Message for Each Day," were originally prepared for the monthly Bible study magazine, *Our Hope*, in which, with only occasional interruption, they have been printed ever since. Several years ago they began to appear in *The Presbyterian* at the suggestion of its Editor, the Rev. Stewart M. Robinson, D.D.; and in the spring of 1938 their publication in *The Christian Observer* was undertaken, also by request of its Editor, the Rev. William T. McElroy, D.D. Thus the Daily Messages are at present reaching a section of the Christian public estimated at between 40,000 and 50,000 subscribers. Through letters and also through spoken comment of readers from widely separated parts of the country it has become evident that these little paragraphs have been spiritually helpful to individuals. The collection of some of them in permanent form has therefore seemed advisable.

Whatever the following pages may mean to their readers, there is no doubt of the fact that their preparation has been of immeasurable blessing to the one who has written them. To turn to the Bible time and again for the express purpose of finding some truth worthy of sharing with others, thus to write close to two thousand different messages, and yet never to be disappointed in the Book, is an unforgettable experience of the inexhaustibility of the Word of God. The author is sensible of the inadequacy of much that he has set down. Yet he must say that a good part of it has come from his own experience, as, looking unto Christ, he has sought to exalt Him through ministering

PREFACE

to the devotional life of his readers. If the Messages contain something of rebuke, that rebuke has been first of all directed to their writer; if they express thanksgiving, he has shared it; and if they are conducive to greater love for the Saviour, it is because their author, deeply conscious of his own shortcoming, has endeavored to pay tribute to the Lord of Glory.

The matter of arrangement has been a problem. After weighing the relative merits of topical arrangement and presentation according to Scriptural occurrence, the author decided upon the present order. In working it out he has aimed at one thing—diversity. After all, the needs of users of a book such as this are unpredictable, and any rigid order might decrease its utility in meeting individual needs. All things considered, it has therefore seemed best to seek the greatest possible variety. For those readers, however, who wish to refer back to various messages or follow through the Scripture order of passages treated an index is provided.

To his friend, Dr. E. Schuyler English of Philadelphia, the author is indebted for invaluable aid, given with characteristic graciousness, in seeing this book through the press. Grateful acknowledgment is also made to James Clarke and Company of London for permission to quote from Weymouth's translation of the New Testament, and to the International Council of Religious Education of Chicago for permission to quote from the American Standard Edition of the Revised Bible.

FRANK E. GAEBELEIN

Stony Brook, Long Island
1941

PREFACE
To the New Edition

OF ALL MY BOOKS, none is closer to my heart than this selection of devotional comments on passages of Scripture. Most of it was written in the midst of the crowded life of a boys' school. As I look back over the messages, there come to mind many of the circumstances out of which they grew. The truths set down in these pages reflect what the texts on which they are based meant to me at the time of their writing. As I have re-read them, I have been impressed with the fact that the lessons we gain from God's Word as we seek its meaning for us do not wear out. I am aware of the inadequacy of my attempts to state Christian truth in clear and helpful form. Yet I am also persuaded of the full adequacy of the Lord Jesus Christ, who is the center of Scripture and whose life is communicated to us through the Bible.

Although this book has been out of print for a number of years, calls for it have continued. The publisher has therefore decided to bring out this new edition. It is my hope that, as these daily messages from God's Word continue in circulation, they may communicate to their readers something of the help they have brought their writer.

FRANK E. GAEBELEIN

The Stony Brook School
Stony Brook, Long Island
October, 1961

Unto him that loved us, and washed
us from our sins in his own blood . . .
— Revelation 1:5

JANUARY 1

De not conformed to this world: but be ye transformed by the renewing of your mind (Rom. 12: 2).

Non-conformity to the world and its ways, transformation through a new mind, these are the ideals with which Paul confronts the Romans as he pleads for their surrender to God. At the beginning of another year we may well face this earnest exhortation and ask ourselves a few direct questions. Are we prepared to be non-conformists, conscientious objectors to the world? Are we willing to be thought different, to stand alone for the sake of Christ? Is our great heart hunger for a complete transformation (the Greek means "life-change") into the image of Christ? Above all do we really want a renewed mind, an outlook upon life that is steadily less of the world and more of Christ? All these can be yours and mine, not through striving, but through obedience to the will of God for us as we abide in the Lord Jesus.

JANUARY 2

And He that hath sent Me is with Me: the Father hath not left Me alone; for I do always those things that please Him (John 8: 29).

What a claim! "I do always those things that please Him." But that stupendous claim of a life completely pleasing in every last detail to the will of God could be safely made by the Lord Jesus. For the Father's testimony to His Son at His baptism, "This is My beloved Son in Whom I am well pleased" (Matt. 3:17), was repeated toward the close of His earthly ministry, when on the Mount of Transfiguration God again spoke from Heaven saying, "This is My beloved Son, in Whom I am well pleased; hear ye Him" (Matt. 17:5).

"I do always those things that please Him." Think of the implications of those words. They mean not a single selfish deed, not one unhallowed word, no unrighteousness of any kind. For God is holy and nothing unholy in thought, word, or deed could ever be pleasing to Him. Oh, Christian, does not your heart bow in adoration as you contemplate the perfection of your Lord's character?

JANUARY 3

Accept, I beseech Thee, the freewill-offerings of my mouth, O Lord (Ps. 119:108).

How sad that there is among Christians so comparatively little of this kind of free-will offering! The reason is that the Lord occupies but a small part of our conversation. Doubtless the Psalmist had public worship in mind, yet his striking phrase suggests far more than public worship. To a God who has done so exceeding abundantly above all we ask or even think we offer singularly little praise. If our tongues do turn to spiritual topics, it is often to doctrinal disputation or personal criticism of some church or servant of the Lord.

Have you ever thought of what might happen in your life, if you were to devote one-tenth of your *words* as free-will offerings in thanksgiving for God's marvelous grace to you through the Lord Jesus Christ? Would not the windows of Heaven be opened to pour down their spiritual blessings upon your life?

JANUARY 4

We know not what we should pray for as we ought: but the Spirit Himself maketh intercession for us with groanings which cannot be uttered (Rom. 8: 26).

"And," continues Paul, "He that searcheth the hearts knoweth what is the mind of the Spirit, because He maketh intercession for the saints according to the will of God" (vs. 27). Surely these are two of the most comforting verses in all Scripture. They are comforting because they meet such a universal need in prayer. Sometimes the load is so crushing and the anguish so great that we are speechless. We kneel and reach out dumbly to God. Ah, then is the time when we may be sure of being heard. For then is the time when our prayers are ascending perfectly to our Heavenly Father. There is One by our side to help, even the Holy Spirit of God. He is our divine Interpreter, and the great Searcher of hearts heeds His intercession.

JANUARY 5

Be of good courage, and do it (Ezra 10:4).

To be sure, you may be faced right now with a very difficult thing. But if it is God's will for you, it *must* be done. And the only way to do it is to take the simple advice of this verse. There come times, you see, when even prayer will not suffice. God is demanding something else. Woe to you, if, when God calls to action, you just continue to wait before Him. It is just as much against the will of God to pray when He would have you do something, as it is not to pray when He would have you on your knees. Indecision in the face of unpleasant duty is all too common among Christians. No matter what God calls you to do today, "Be of good courage, and do it."

JANUARY 6

My grace is sufficient for thee: for My strength is made perfect in weakness (II Cor. 12:9).

There are many places in the Bible not for the bold and self-assured and this is one of them. If you are confident in your own strength, this text is not for you. But if you realize your insufficiency, then God can speak to you through these inspired words written by His servant Paul. They apply to those who are burdened with problems beyond their power to solve, who face tasks too great for their strength, who are suffering afflictions that cannot be remedied. To all such they bring the self-same assurance that encouraged Paul, for they say that God's grace *is* sufficient for the weak and the burdened and the afflicted. They certify that the perfection of His strength shines forth in our human weakness.

Let us never be ashamed of owning up to our weakness. If so great a man as the Apostle Paul did not hesitate to acknowledge his weakness, no more need we. Our most perilous times are the times of our human strength. Paul expressed the paradox of spiritual safety when he wrote, "When I am weak, then am I strong" (vs. 10).

JANUARY 7

Fear not: believe only (Luke 8:50).

There is no more destructive emotion than fear. Within bounds it has its place as a deterrent from evil. But once let it break loose, and it can paralyze life and ruin peace of heart and mind. God's Word never makes false emphases, and therefore it is definitely significant that over and over again the Bible speaks against fear. Witness our Lord's frequent teaching on the subject, as in these four precious words which we are to treasure in our hearts for today.

Do you know what Christ's most difficult command is? Simply this: "Fear not." There come times in life when fear may lay hold on one with a grip that mere will-power cannot shake. Well, those are the times to apply the greatest soul medicine ever prescribed: "only believe." Oh, that we might in our darkest moments turn to the great Physician, and apply His remedy to our souls! Fear is the enemy of faith, but faith always vanquishes fear. "Fear not; believe only."

JANUARY 8

And as he lay and slept under a juniper tree, behold, then an angel touched him, and said unto him, Arise and eat (I Kings 19:5).

"As he lay and slept . . . *then* an angel." It is a precious thought of God's unceasing care that this verse brings us. Elijah, bold before multitudes, has run away from a woman. Worn out and discouraged, he hides in the wilderness. But while he sleeps the Lord is active in his behalf. The incident is small, but its implications large. It assures us that there is never a time in a believer's life when God is not active in his behalf. When we are worn out and discouraged, *then* God sends the angel of mercy; when we are hungry and destitute, *then* He sets a table in the wilderness. And so, even when we reach some place of utter weakness, let us not hesitate to take our rest. The same Lord Who sent the angel to minister to Elijah will not fail to watch over us.

JANUARY 9

*He calleth His own sheep by name, and leadeth them
out* (John 10:3).

It is a very blessed aspect of our redemption that our relationship to the Good Shepherd of the sheep is so completely
personal. He calls us not en masse, but individually and by
name. He leads us in and out one by one. Though we all belong to that great fold which is His heart, yet each sheep has
its own special place within that fold. When we stumble and
fall, His loving arms lift us up and restore us one by one
to His tender bosom. It is not self-centeredness but the deep
joy of Christian security which leads us to sing the simple
old song, "I am so glad that Jesus loves me . . . Jesus loves
even me."

JANUARY 10

*I know the things that come into your mind, every one
of them* (Ezek. 11:5).

Perhaps this arresting statement of God's complete knowledge of our thought-life will help us to greater spiritual
honesty. It is not enough when it comes to meeting the divine
standard, to be technically righteous. If God knows everything that comes into our minds, He knows our sins of
thought, as well as of act. He is aware of the sinful things
we should have liked to have done, but out of fear of detec-
tion or of consequences, have only cherished in our minds.
He knows the hidden indulgences that, though confined to
thought, are still blameworthy in His sight. No man, realizing
these and similar things, can ever have the least hesitation
in acknowledging himself a sinner in the sight of a holy God.

But there is another aspect of this matter. God, Who sees
everything that comes into our minds, is not responsible for
all of these things. He knows the temptations and the fears
which the enemy insinuates into our thinking; He realizes
their source. And when He finds a mind that, though assailed
by the Tempter, is yet resisting the Tempter's assaults, He
helps that one with the irresistible power of His perfect love.
Because God knows all about us, even unto every one of our
thoughts, He only understands us fully. Because He only
understands us fully, He alone is able completely to help
us at all times.

JANUARY 11

Let us therefore come boldly unto the throne of grace, that we may obtain mercy, and find grace to help in time of need (Heb. 4:16).

"Boldly!" It is doubtful whether there could be a more daring word in relation to man's approach to God. There is no hint in this word of brash presumption or arrogant irreverence. But its meaning is the tremendous one that we Christians may approach the throne of the Almighty Ruler of the universe with free utterance as those who have a right to stand there. Christ gives us that freedom and that right; through Him we approach the throne as blood-bought children of Him Who sits upon it. It means that when we believers go before God's throne in prayer we are standing right where we belong and we may speak all that is in our hearts. Oh, that we might go there more often and stay there longer!

JANUARY 12

Be patient toward all men (I Thess. 5:14).

Shortness of temper, so often condoned among us Christians as a mere defect of disposition, has no justification in view of this verse and others like it. Notice how sweeping Paul's exhortation is, applying as it does to *all* men. If there are times when even our best loved cause us to lose patience, how much more careful must we be in our relation to those outside the small circle of our dear ones.

"To lose patience." How common the phrase, and how little it troubles us! We get "out of patience," and think that our lapse is dealt with by a verbal shrug of the shoulder. But all the time the fact remains that we have boldly flouted an express command of Scripture.

Patience is God-like, for God is unspeakably forbearing in His dealings with us. Patience was preëminently exhibited by the Lord Jesus Christ, Who "endured such contradiction of sinners against Himself." And shall we fail to cultivate this virtue which God so highly values?

JANUARY 13

I have seen his ways and will heal him (Isa. 57:18).

God is the only perfect healer, for God alone is omniscient. Just as a medical cure depends upon accurate diagnosis of the disease, so our soul's health can only be maintained by Him Who sees us through and through.

Do not be afraid, O Christian, of God's searching gaze. He Who looks deep down into your innermost heart is your loving Heavenly Father. When His eye meets a bad spot, His purpose is always to make it right. Like the perfect Physician that He is, He never sees a sick soul without desiring its healing. What then, if He uses the scalpel of chastening or the probe of sorrow? He Who has "seen our ways" says, "I will heal" you.

JANUARY 14

Be filled with the Spirit (Eph. 5:18).

This is a positive command, not an optional suggestion. Using the imperative, the inspired apostle enjoins Christians to be filled with the Spirit. Now that plain fact implies that it is possible for us believers not to be filled with the Spirit. And it asks each of us these questions: "Am I filled with the Spirit? If not, why?" For Paul is describing the walk of the Christian. Evidently for him the Spirit-filled life was the normal rather than the abnormal thing. How sad, therefore, that so many today have reversed the Word of God to the extent of looking upon a truly Spirit-filled Christian as some rare and holy phenomenon to be wondered at but hardly emulated by the rank and file.

"Be filled with the Spirit." If words mean anything, this implies that you and I can be Spirit-filled. When we believed, Christ came to dwell in our hearts through the Holy Spirit. The filling of the Spirit is His full possession of our lives; full surrender is what leads to Spirit-filling. If we are not filled, it is never the fault of the Holy Spirit. He always wants to indwell Christian hearts in all His fulness, but He cannot occupy territory unsurrendered to Him. He cannot fill hearts already half full of self and sin and worldliness.

JANUARY 15

We have seen His star in the east, and are come to worship Him (Matt. 2:2).

There is much spiritual logic in these words of the wise men. They had seen Christ's star; therefore they came to worship Him. So must it always be when men see Christ in any way. Beholding the Saviour means adoring Him. And conversely, if your spiritual life is deficient in worship, you may need to see Christ anew. The wise men beheld only His star; but you have the Word of God, and in that Word you may see with the eye of faith a full length portrait of the Lord Jesus. You also have prayer, and in prayer He makes Himself known; and you have service as well, and to those who pour themselves out in sacrificial service for others He has His special revelation. Christ does not hide Himself from anyone who truly longs to see and worship Him.

JANUARY 16

Thou hast holden me by my right hand (Ps. 73:23).

As an exceedingly terse expression of divine guidance, this sentence merits meditation. Its unique message lies in the single adjective which it contains. "Thou hast holden me," writes the Psalmist Asaph, "by my *right* hand." Now the right hand is the administrative hand. It is the hand of power. And when God holds us by our right hand, He takes full control of our lives.

In his literal translation Dr. Young renders the verse in this way, thereby bringing out a significant shade of meaning: "Thou hast *laid hold* on my right hand." It is one thing to have God lay hold of your right hand; it is another thing to submit your right hand to God's grasp. The trouble with some of us is that when God takes our right hands, we pull the other way. If we would only submit our hands to His, if we would learn to realize that in our darkest hours our God is securely holding our right hands, we should know more of the blessing of His perfect guidance.

JANUARY 17

We have this treasure in earthen vessels, that the excellency of the power may be of God, and not of us (II Cor. 4:7).

The next time you begin to bewail your human weakness, just look at this verse. Learn from it that God delights to use your littleness, for it makes clear beyond a shadow of a doubt that the source of your power is from God and not from you. You are an earthen vessel, and you were made an earthen vessel by the all-wise Potter. Cease, then, from complaining, and marvel that He is willing to manifest the excellency of His power in you. You will be much happier if you will accept your limitations, not with passive lamenting, but with expectant faith that looks to God to transmute a vessel of clay into an instrument for the accomplishment of His glorious purpose.

JANUARY 18

Men ought always to pray, and not to faint (Luke 18:1).

We often speak of the privilege of prayer. But, though prayer is undoubtedly a very great spiritual privilege, there is something misleading in thus designating it. For the word "privilege" rather implies option. And prayer is in no sense optional for the Christian; it is a duty and a responsibility. Thus our Lord uses the word of strong obligation when He says, "Men *ought* always to pray."

Did it ever occur to you that prayer is not listed among the gifts of the Spirit? Teaching, prophecy, exhortation, ministering—these are among the special enduements which the Spirit confers upon His instruments. Why, then, is prayer not among them? Prayer is not among them because it is the common possession and duty of every believer. We *all* have access to God the Father through the Lord Jesus Christ. And if your prayer life is not what it should be, do not offer the lame excuse that you do not have any gift for prayer. Just be honest. Tell the Lord Jesus that you have neglected your essential obligation to pray, and then ask Him to teach you to pray. He will do it even as He taught His disciples to pray.

JANUARY 19

Keep thyself pure (I Tim. 5: 22).

Personal responsibility underlies these words. Purity is not a once-and-for-all matter. It needs to be maintained. The whitest hand must constantly be washed, the fairest linen must be kept white by soap and water. So with ourselves. Cleansed by the blood of Christ, we nevertheless contract new defilement from an impure world. Just how much sullied we become depends in real measure upon us. God has given us the power of choice. We can stay apart from evil persons and evil things. It is possible for us to keep ourselves pure, if our purity be the result of a moment by moment reliance upon Christ.

JANUARY 20

Whosoever committeth sin is the slave of sin (John 8:34).

We have all heard and used the phrase, "a self-made man," although in strict accuracy there is no such thing. Yet, whether there be a completely self-made man or not, there is certainly many a self-made slave. Even a democracy such as our America is full of slaves. For Christ says that whosoever is habitually committing sin is the slave of that very sin which he is committing. Such a one is a self-made slave. Yielding himself to some unholy practice, he soon finds himself bound with unbreakable chains of his own manufacture to the things he loathes.

Let us not make the mistake of so many religious people in considering ourselves above the possibility of falling into this dreadful bondage. Christ nowhere confines slavery to the grosser sins. In His holy eyes there is little difference between being a vassal to drink and a slave to a mean disposition or a gossiping tongue. In either case the state is one of bondage to the self-forged shackles of our sin. What we need, therefore, is to recognize in Christ not only our Saviour from the guilt and penalty of sins that are past, but also our Emancipator from sins that are crippling our service by holding some portion of our lives in thrall.

JANUARY 21

They shall fight against thee, but they shall not prevail against thee: for I am with thee, saith Jehovah, to deliver thee (Jer. 1:19, A.S.V.).

With these words God encouraged the heart of the youthful Jeremiah when he was called to prophesy. This message is not a transitory one; God encourages ancient prophet and present-day believer in the same way. He Whose Name is "I AM THAT I AM" is timeless. He Who said to young Jeremiah, "I am with thee," encourages us today. We do not have to be prophets to be called of God. Every single believer is called, specially and directly, by the Heavenly Father. And therefore every believer may claim the promise that the enemy of his soul will never prevail against him, for Jehovah is still saying, "I am with thee to deliver thee."

JANUARY 22

And when the day of Pentecost was fully come, they were all with one accord in one place (Acts 2:1).

"All with one accord in one place." We see by these few words that the Holy Spirit came into an atmosphere of unity and harmony. It is more than doubtful if He would have come, had there been dissension and strife among the waiting disciples. The preliminary to the descent of the Holy Spirit in heavenly power was a unitedly waiting Church. This is not an argument for the kind of church union that too often is based upon compromise of vital truth. But it does constitute a forceful plea for the unity of believers, as together they seek the power of the Holy Spirit. It is thus that revivals come to communities. It is thus that individual churches and institutions find new power. When those who are like-minded in the Lord will take the time to wait unitedly before Him, He will speak in power. Although the special supernatural manifestations of Pentecost were for that day only, the same Holy Spirit is for this day and every day. And, when hearts are believingly and patiently and unitedly waiting for Him, He will come in power at God's appointed time.

JANUARY 23

When Jesus saw their faith . . . (Mark 2:5).

Seeing faith? Yes, that is exactly what the Lord Jesus did; He saw the unseen faith in the hearts of four men. If you will read the preceding verses, you will see that these four men insisted upon bringing their palsied friend into the presence of Christ, despite the thronging crowd. So they ascended the roof, uncovered it, and let their friend down before the Lord. And that was the faith which Christ saw. He saw four men acting upon the assumption that He was able to help their afflicted friend. The obstacles were very real; their friend was helpless; the thronging crowd prevented the usual access to Christ. But the four were not deterred. They went ahead against the difficulties, trusting in the ability of the Lord Jesus. And that was and is faith—*simply acting upon the assumption that Jesus is able.* The Lord always sees that kind of faith. And when He sees it, He always honors it.

JANUARY 24

He that covereth a transgression seeketh love; but he that repeateth a matter separateth friends (Prov. 17:9).

To cover a transgression is divine for that is what God has done for the sinner. Ever since He made the coats of skin for our guilty parents in Eden, He has been covering transgressions. And in the blood of Christ He has given sinful humanity the perfect provision that hides even the most dreadful iniquities of those who believe. So it is God-like and Christ-like for you and me to cover the transgressions of our friends. But this does not mean shutting our eyes to them nor does it mean condoning them; God does not deal thus with sin. It simply means forgiving others for Christ's sake, as He has forgiven us. It simply means refusing to dwell upon, and gloat over, and pass on as a savory morsel of gossip the story of some poor soul's downfall. By the presence of this God-like quality true Christians become beloved and trusted; by its absence they cause divisions and offenses, even in the household of faith.

JANUARY 25

I will surely do thee good (Gen. 32:12).

What a foundation on which to live today! What a joy to say, as did Jacob in his prayer, "Thou hast said, I will surely do thee good"! With that assurance in the heart, nothing can daunt the trusting child of God. Our Father's intention toward His children is *always* good. If we are tempted to doubt that, we need only to remember the length to which His love went in redeeming us through the blood of His only-begotten Son.

JANUARY 26

Though I walk through the valley of the shadow of death, I will fear no evil (Ps. 23:4).

Few things can be more terrifying than a certain kind of shadow; yet in itself every shadow is harmless. Its terror lies only in the fact that it points to a reality behind it. But shadows do not tell the truth; they have a way of distorting objects, and they can on occasion turn something quite harmless into a sinister spectre. Thus children learn, as they grow up, not to be afraid of the shadows of the dusk, for experience has shown them that shadows lie.

Now if we could but treat the shadows of the spirit in somewhat the same way, how much happier we should be. One of Satan's favorite devices is to cast shadows upon us—shadows of impending calamity, of sickness, of failure, of death itself. Yes, they reflect real things; there is something behind them. But, coming as they do from the evil one, they are all, without exception, lying shadows distorted so as to strike fear into the hearts of God's people.

For this fear of shadows, God has given us the antidote in the inspired words of the Psalmist: "Though I walk through the valley of the shadow of death, I will fear no evil; for Thou art with me." Death is indeed real. But it is not for the Christian the horrible shadow into which Satan has distorted it. With the Shepherd Saviour by your side, the valley of shadows, even of death, may become a time of sweetest fellowship. Perfect love does indeed cast out fear.

JANUARY 27

Exceeding great and precious promises (II Peter 1: 4).

Do you know the promises of God? The fact that so many believers are unfamiliar with the divine promises has much to do with their feebleness in prayer. From Genesis to Revelation the Bible is full of promises from our Heavenly Father, and every one of them is guaranteed by the holy integrity of our God. For, as the author of Hebrews says, "It is impossible for God to lie."

You may be absolutely certain that somewhere in Scripture there is a promise from God precisely fitted to your every need. To be very definite in prayer honors the Heavenly Father. One of the assured avenues for prevailing prayer is to go before the Lord with some specific promise from His Word, to apply that promise in exact accord with its meaning, and then just to rest upon the immutable fact that a faithful God can never be unfaithful to His pledged Word.

JANUARY 28

Now when Daniel knew that the writing was signed, he went into his house; and his windows being open in his chamber toward Jerusalem, he kneeled upon his knees three times a day, and prayed, and gave thanks before his God, as he did aforetime (Dan. 6:10).

The perilous circumstances that hemmed Daniel in are too well known to need recounting. And his response to them will never lose its value as an example of what real godliness means. Knowing full well the plot of his enemies, he did not hesitate to seal his doom by continuing to pray.

Let us take to our hearts one significant phrase from our verse for today. The record says that Daniel "gave thanks before his God, as he did aforetime." In other words nothing could disturb the prayer habits of Daniel. In the face of the most extreme peril he kept right on giving thanks, "as he did aforetime." It is a great thing to learn, as Daniel learned, to give thanks to God always and in all circumstances.

JANUARY 29

Teaching us that, denying ungodliness and worldly lusts, we should live soberly, righteously, and godly in this present world (Titus 2:12).

Here we plainly see the purpose of Christ's incarnation in relation to our lives. For in the preceding verse Paul describes in these words the coming of the Lord Jesus into the world: "the grace of God that bringeth salvation hath appeared to all men." And in our text for today he shows that the purpose of this incarnate appearance of the grace of God is our instruction in all forms of godly living. That being the case, let us draw some conclusions. It is never a matter of small moment for any Christian to be living in an ungodly way. For when a Christian tolerates evil and selfishness in his life, he is harboring things that would defeat the very purpose of his Lord's incarnation. And no one can do that with impunity; God must deal in chastisement with lives that thus dishonor Him.

JANUARY 30

Looking for that blessed hope and the glorious appearing of the great God and our Saviour Jesus Christ (Titus 2:13).

Would you have the key to living for Christ "in this present world"? Here it is in these two words, "looking for." Expectancy is the key, expectancy that eagerly awaits "that blessed hope" which is nothing less than "the glorious appearing of the great God and our Saviour Jesus Christ." Is there room in your heart for expectant longing for your Lord from Heaven? Then you truly love Him. For no one longs for the appearance of a person who is an object of indifference.

What will Christ's appearing mean? Well, it will mean the establishment of His Kingdom and the consequent end of the present world order. Therefore, expectancy of His coming is both the antidote for the love of the world and the key to righteous and godly living in an evil age.

JANUARY 31

And he said, The Lord is my rock, and my fortress, and my deliverer; the God of my rock, in Him will I trust: He is my shield, and the horn of my salvation, my high tower, and my refuge, my Saviour (II Sam. 22: 2, 3).

At the close of his life, David looks back and sees that "the Lord had delivered him out of the hand of all his enemies, and out of the hand of Saul." Yes, there had been dark places in David's life, places where he had been even in the hand of the arch-enemy, Satan. But in every difficulty David had experienced the faithfulness of God.

Here speaks the real David. If he was "a man after God's heart," the reason for that supreme distinction is shown in one little word. "*My* rock, *my* fortress, *my* deliverer, the God of *my* rock, *my* shield, *my* salvation, *my* high tower, *my* refuge, *my* Saviour!" "My"—that was David's secret. He dared attach the personal, possessive pronoun to the greatness of God. Few generals have ever surpassed David, but he did not come to the close of his life speaking of "my" military powers; few rulers have achieved more than David, but he did not finish his reign pointing to "my" kingdom; no poet has ever surpassed David, but he did not speak of "my" Psalms. No, David was a man after God's own heart, because he realized his own need sufficiently well to cling to the Lord alone with an intensely personal grip nothing could shake. And in that essential thing you and I, though we may be quite without David's other talents, may follow him.

Dear friend, when *the* Lord, *the* Rock, *the* Fortress, and *the* Saviour becomes for you *my* Lord, *my* Rock, *my* Fortress, and *my* Saviour, then you have a faith that can never be shaken.

> *A mighty Fortress is our God,*
> *A Bulwark never failing;*
> *Our Helper He amid the flood*
> *Of mortal ills prevailing.*

FEBRUARY 1

Little children, abide in Him (I John 2:28).

Have you ever reflected upon the extreme simplicity of the essential requirements for the spiritual life? God's Word does not ask us to be deep thinkers, eloquent speakers, or great scholars. For those things would be quite beyond the capacity of all but the very few. But God's Word does require that we should abide in Christ. Now abiding is something that everyone, regardless of his natural gifts can do. The uneducated can abide just as well as the learned; the weak are fully as well qualified to abide as the strong. To abide requires the simple resolution not to be moved from a certain dwelling place, and the believer's dwelling place is Christ. God's primary commands are binding upon all because they are within the capacity of all. Are you abiding in Christ?

FEBRUARY 2

Were there not ten cleansed? But where are the nine? (Luke 17:17).

Only one grateful leper out of ten who were healed! But is the proportion of gratitude any higher among us? Spiritually considered, every Christian is in the place of the cleansed lepers, for just as incurable as leprosy is sin. To be cleansed spiritually is every whit as great a miracle as to be cleansed from leprosy.

But that is not all. The Lord Who loves us and washed us from our sins also watches over us daily. Innumerable are the times when He saves us out of our distresses. With each new day He bestows fresh mercies. From the provision of our daily bread to deliverance from our sorest distress, in sickness and in health, in joy and in sorrow whether we wake or sleep, He is graciously caring for us. Would that more of us were taking the place of the one leper! Would that more of us were going daily before the Lord, not to ask for something, but just to thank Him for what He has done for us! To get down on one's knees and thank God one by one for all His blessings is well-pleasing to His loving heart.

FEBRUARY 3

To God be the thanks Who in Christ ever leads in His triumphal procession . . . (II Cor. 2:14, Weymouth).

The Greek here gives the picture of being led captive in a triumphal procession. So it is with those who in Christ present themselves living sacrifices unto God; they become His willing captives and are given a place in His all-conquering train. Away, then, with the dreary and lugubrious misconceptions of the Christian life! It is a procession, glorious, triumphant, marching on to eternal victory. And it is a procession in the ranks of which every Christian has his place. What though it dip down into the valley of despair and wind through the dark forests of gloom? Its course is onward to triumph, and its great Captain is invincible.

FEBRUARY 4

Is thine heart right? (II Kings 10:15).

This is a question which we should constantly be asking ourselves. "Is my heart right?" Upon my answer to that question, as it reveals the state of my heart toward my Lord, depends all my effectiveness in serving and glorifying Him.

What, then, does it mean to have a heart that is right before God? As we think along this line, we see that the question is not to be glibly answered. This much is plain. There is only one kind of heart that is right in God's sight, and that is the regenerated heart. No one whose heart has not been cleansed by the redeeming blood of Christ is right before God. Yet, though the redeemed heart is judicially right in the sight of God, from the experimental point of view it may be otherwise. When the heart of a believer cherishes some secret sin, when it harbors a grudge, when it grows cold in its love for its Redeemer, when it rests to the slightest degree upon itself and its goodness and not upon Christ, then it is not right. "Is my heart right?" You only, alone with the Lord, can give the answer.

FEBRUARY 5

Grace and peace be multiplied unto you through the knowl-edge of God, and of Jesus our Lord (II Peter 1: 2).

Have you ever thought of God's arithmetic? In this salutation of his valedictory letter Peter speaks of grace and peace being "multiplied" unto those whom he was addressing. It is apparent that Peter is referring to something that should be the normal Christian experience. For there should be in our lives a veritable multiplication of God's grace and peace. If this is not true of us, the reason may well be that we are lacking the one thing through which the divine arithmetic works, which is "the knowledge of God and of Jesus our Lord." It is very doubtful whether Christians who are contentedly ignorant of God's Word and its truth concerning Christ are capable of receiving their share of God's multiplied blessings.

FEBRUARY 6

It is Christ that died (Rom. 8:34).

This is Paul's final answer to the suggestion of condemnation for the believer. And his emphasis is plainly upon the word "Christ." It is not just the death that matters; it is the Person of the One Who died. Everything depends upon the fact that it was the Christ of God Who shed His blood upon the Cross. Because the Son of God died, there can never be any condemnation for those whom He has reconciled to God. What no sinful man could do, however unselfish his martyrdom, Christ accomplished by His atoning death.

"But," says the modern objector, "that is just theology." Yes, it is theology, but it is also one of the most practical facts of the Christian life. The enemy of our souls attacks us. Our answer is the affirmation: "It is Christ that died." Elsewhere Paul urges that we take the shield of faith wherewith we shall be able to quench all the fiery darts of the wicked one. And as we do so, let us have emblazoned on it the invincible truth, "It is Christ that died."

FEBRUARY 7

Justice and judgment are the habitation of Thy throne; mercy and truth shall go before Thy face (Ps. 89:14).

Nowhere in Scripture is the precise location of the heavenly throne given. The exact place where God dwells is not revealed. But what is not told us materially is made known morally. For this verse clearly shows the moral location of God's throne. "Justice and judgment are the habitation of Thy throne; mercy and truth shall go before Thy face." Neither east nor west, north nor south, limit God's presence. But when it comes to moral and spiritual things, there are places where God cannot dwell. He cannot dwell where there are injustice and false judgment where cruelty and falsehood hold sway. He cannot have His throne amid any form of sin. Let us remember this as we seek to yield our lives to God and present our hearts as the habitation of the Holy Spirit of Christ.

FEBRUARY 8

Go to the ant, thou sluggard, consider her ways, and be wise: which having no guide, overseer, or ruler, provideth her meat in the summer, and gathereth her food in the harvest (Prov. 6:6-8).

Ever since Solomon wrote these words the ant has been held up as the model of industry. But without detracting from that lesson, let us think of another aspect of this extraordinary creature's life. The ant, the proverb tells us, works hard and farsightedly, "having no guide, overseer, or ruler." Therein lies one of its most remarkable and frequently overlooked virtues. For the test of industry is not working under direction, but working voluntarily. You work hard when your employer is looking, when you are under direction. All very well, but that does not mean that you are industrious. Would you work hard, were no employer watching? That is the real test. And it constitutes one of the great pitfalls of Christian service, wherein the worker is so often under the direction of no man. May God deliver us from sloth by making us conscious of the fact that there is One Who is watching us and waiting to direct us in our spiritual labor.

FEBRUARY 9

My sheep listen to My voice (John 10. 27, Weymouth).

You claim to be one of His sheep. But do you really listen to His voice? Do you know His voice well enough to distinguish it among the distracting noises of the world and the clamor of self?

Our Lord, that great Shepherd of the sheep, speaks in certain definite ways to His own. He speaks through His Word, in prayer, and by circumstances of His arranging. If you would hear Him, you must be close to Him and walking with Him. Be it said reverently, He never raises His voice; He speaks firmly, insistently, but quietly. May God grant us single hearts and attentive ears that will listen to His sweet words!

FEBRUARY 10

Jesus said to them, Have faith in God (Mark 11: 22).

Hudson Taylor of China, who probably knew more about effectual prayer than any Christian of modern times, is said to have used this suggestive translation of our text for today, "Hold fast God's faithfulness." And, according to Dr. and Mrs. Howard Taylor, he would say by way of comment: "It is not so much *great* faith that we need as faith in a *great* God." The distinction may seem subtle, yet it is vastly important. Answered prayer depends upon God's inexhaustible power whereby He is abundantly able to be faithful to His pledged Word. It is our privilege simply to reckon upon the unchangeable reliability of our omnipotent God, believing that He not only can, but also will do all that He has promised. But surely "privileged" is too weak a word. For the Lord Jesus used the verb form which expresses a command. *"Have faith in God,"* He said. So He is telling us Christian believers that we have an imperative obligation to be just what our name implies—*believers*. Will you not be enough of a believer to "hold fast God's faithfulness" in everything that faces you this day?

FEBRUARY 11

So there was a division of the people concerning Him
(John 7:43).

Christ did not come to make us merely comfortable. His
presence and message are disturbing to much that we value.
The preaching of His Gospel always divides. Even in the individual life this is true. When Christ enters our hearts, lines
must be drawn. Unsanctified associations and doubtful practices have to go. For the proclamation of Gospel truth to
leave all who hear it in a state of placidity is the sign that
something is wrong with the preacher or the hearer. Wherever Christ is, there the dividing process is going on. Is He
at work in your life, dividing the good from the evil, the holy
from the unholy, the carnal from the spiritual?

FEBRUARY 12

*Blessed is he whose transgression is forgiven, whose sin is
covered* (Ps. 32:1).

Among all the Scripture beatitudes this one is fundamental.
Antecedent to every kind of blessing that man may experience
is this blessedness of the forgiven transgression and the
covered sin. The very form of words in which it is expressed
has its message of redeeming grace. "Blessed is he," exclaimed David, using the passive voice of the verbs "whose
transgression *is forgiven,* whose sin *is covered.*" This blessedness is therefore not a result of human effort; the forgiveness is unearned, the sin covered by God and not by man.
But let us notice also the solemn fact that, apart from this
primary beatitude of redemption, no true blessing can come
to any soul. For he whose transgression is unforgiven, whose
sin lies open to the sight of the holy One, can only be under
God's curse. Oh, may God show us believers all over again
that the source of our every blessing is the dying love of our
Saviour! And may unbelievers be delivered from that snare
whereby, with unforgiven transgressions and uncovered sin,
they are deluding themselves with counterfeit blessings. No
forgiveness, no blessing! That is the uniform principle behind all spiritual benefits.

FEBRUARY 13

Kings and priests unto God (Rev. 1:6).

It is by no means without significance that these words, so expressive of the exalted privileges of the believer's priesthood, are part of a great doxology. At the beginning of His inspired unveiling of the glories of Christ, John ascribes "glory and dominion for ever and ever . . . unto Him that loved us, and washed us from our sins in His own blood, and *hath made us kings and priests unto God and His Father.*" Christians are indeed priests. They have access to the very throne of grace. They are a royal priesthood, for they are fellow-heirs with the Son Himself. But—they are priests *unto God*. The purpose of their priesthood is not just to acquire things for themselves and others; it is rather to glorify God. Very beautifully does the Lord Jesus show that in His high priestly prayer (John 17), the ground tone of which is God's glory. That prayer contains very definite petitions, but they are all bound up with the Father's glory.

When we Christians learn to relate our intercessory prayers to the Father's glory, when we realize that we are priests *unto God* and not unto our own desires alone, then we shall experience a greater release of God's power through prayer.

FEBRUARY 14

I will instruct thee and teach thee in the way which thou shalt go: I will guide thee with Mine eye (Ps. 32:8).

Surely this is a verse of marvelous comfort! But not everyone comes under its blessed provisions. It is addressed to one class of people only—the teachable. It is not God's willingness to instruct and guide His children that is in question; it is their willingness to be taught of Him and shown the way. One thing above all else blocks our Lord's leading of us, and that is self-occupation. Oh, we may think we are very humble and spiritual and sacrificial. But so long as we are occupied with ourselves, the Good Shepherd cannot lead us. When we look away from Him we lose the way. He wills to guide us with His eyes upon us; our part is just to turn our eyes toward Him.

FEBRUARY 15

He is altogether lovely (Song of Sol. 5:16).

We Christians know far too little about meditation upon the Person of our Lord. Were more of our prayer time to be spent in quietly thinking of Him instead of in petition alone, were we to search the Word daily to learn of Him instead of looking only for things that we think might immediately help us in our own concerns, we should have a higher appreciation of the loveliness of Christ. Says the author of the Epistle to the Hebrews, "Consider Christ Jesus." Just a little time of daily meditation upon Him will do more to revive our spiritual lives than anything else. For it is impossible to behold Christ without loving Him, and it is impossible to love Him without serving Him.

FEBRUARY 16

I will not leave you orphans (John 14:18, Margin).

What a blessed word of assurance from the Lord Jesus Himself! It is our guarantee that whatever happens, it is absolutely certain that we shall never be forsaken by our Lord. Some things are spiritually impossible, and one of them is for a single Christian soul ever to be deserted. The Lord has given to every believer His pledged word according to that precious Scripture in Hebrews 13:5, "I will never leave thee, nor forsake thee."

And why could Christ, so soon to depart out of this world through the way of the Cross—why could Christ so definitely promise that His disciples, though bereft of His bodily presence, would not be orphans? Every saved soul should know the answer, for every saved soul has the witness of the Holy Spirit, the Comforter Who abides with us forever, even the eternal Spirit of the Lord Jesus Christ. Yes, Christians may be called upon to suffer much for their Lord; they may lose possessions and even their dearest relatives. But God will never put them in a place of separation from the Lord Jesus, for He has promised not to leave them orphans, and His own Spirit dwells forever in the believing heart.

FEBRUARY 17

Peter, however, explained the whole matter to them from the beginning (Acts 11: 4, Weymouth).

The lesson here is simple and practical. Peter had returned to Jerusalem after his vision of the sheet and his ministry to the Gentile, Cornelius, and his household. Quite naturally there was questioning of this new step and "the party of the circumcision found fault with him." All the elements of a bitter misunderstanding were present, but contention was averted. "Peter explained the whole matter to them from the beginning." The result? "On hearing this they were silenced, and they extolled the goodness of God . . ." (vs. 18). Yes, it is an obvious lesson, but one much needed. When contention arises, then take the time patiently to explain things. Nine tenths of our quarrels come from misunderstanding and can be reconciled by the simple and Christian method of patient explanation.

FEBRUARY 18

Who teacheth like Him? (Job 36: 22).

Let this question direct our thoughts to the Lord as our Teacher. How surpassing is His preëminence in this as in all other respects! Men teach out of limited and fallible knowledge; He teaches out of the treasures of His infinite wisdom. Men have only a certain amount of patience; the Lord's patience is limited only by His love, and His love is boundless. Again, men teach mostly by words and acts, but God alone is unlimited in His ability to teach by circumstances. He controls the very lives of His pupils. Whatever happens to them, He is able to use it for their instruction and growth in His knowledge and grace.

The Lord is indeed a matchless Teacher. But are you enrolled in the school of His discipleship? There is but one way to enter that School—by birth. Only those who are born again by faith in the divine Saviour-Teacher are qualified to be His pupils, guided by His watchful eye, instructed daily out of His infinite wisdom.

FEBRUARY 19

*My covenant will I not break, nor alter the thing that is
gone out of My lips* (Ps. 89:34).

Thus does God speak of His solemn covenant with His
servant David. The words, however, rooted as they are in
the immutable fidelity of Almighty God, reach out beyond
the one covenant and embrace all the divine promises. They
assure us that God is not as a man. Once He makes a promise,
it is unalterable, whether it be to David or to all the household of faith, as in the great words of assurance with which
Scripture abounds. Yes, God does mean what He says. There
is blessing in taking Him at His Word.

FEBRUARY 20

*In His love He chose us as His own in Christ . . . that
we might be holy and without blemish in His presence*
(Eph. 1: 4, Weymouth).

What a glorious statement of God's all wise purpose in
calling us believers to be His own children! It tells us
that He chose us for a very special purpose, which is that
"we might be holy and without blemish in His presence."
Now God's choice is obviously the expression of His will.
And, just as nothing can ever deflect the divine will, so nothing can prevent the believer from one day being "holy and
without blemish" in God's presence. Whatever be the im-
perfections of this present life, salvation is the perfect work
of Christ. Thus we can look forward to nothing less than
being clothed upon with His righteousness and being conformed wholly into His glorious image.

But our verse has also its present application. It gives
us not only a glorious hope, but an incentive to holy living
here and now. It indeed assures us of our ultimate perfection in Christ, and at the same time places upon us the obligation to be holy today. For this day and every day we are
in God's presence. And He Who "chose us as His own in
Christ" would have us begin now to be "holy and without
blemish" in His presence. O Christian, are you becoming a
more holy person? Are you letting the Spirit of Christ conform you daily into your Lord's image?

FEBRUARY 21

But the woman . . . fell down before Him, and told Him all the truth (Mark 5: 33).

It is the poor woman afflicted with the issue of blood who is before the Lord Jesus in this instance. When she came into His presence, she not only fell down before Him, but she also told Him all the truth about the thing that was troubling her. And so she teaches us that there are occasions when it is not enough to fall down and worship Christ. If we would have Him lay His hand upon us for the solution of our problems and removal of our burdens, we must do more; we must tell Him *all* the truth. Just as it is folly not to be honest about your sickness with your physician, so is it foolish to refuse to be candid with your Lord. Christ will deal with all of your troubles, but you must first tell them all to Him.

FEBRUARY 22

Render to Caesar the things that are Caesar's, and to God the things that are God's (Mark 12:17).

It is possible to accept the very words of Scripture yet woefully to misapply them. Consider, for instance, this familiar verse. How often many of those who believe it have done violence to its truth, not by denial of that truth, but simply by misplaced emphasis. The danger is not that Caesar will fail to get his due, especially when we take the broader view that Caesar stands for obligations not only to the state but also to mundane things in general. No, the danger is that God will not get *His* due. There are all too many of us Christians who are scrupulously exact about tax-paying and all our business transactions, even to the extent of feeling a glow of self-satisfaction in our detailed devotion to these duties. But how about God? Are we rendering to Him what is His—of our money, of our time, and of our hearts? Are we rendering to Him even one-half hour a day for prayer and meditation?

FEBRUARY 23

My flesh and my heart faileth: but God is the strength of my heart (Ps. 73: 26).

While the failure of the flesh and the heart is always a distressing experience, it ought never to be a surprise to any Christian. For Scripture tells us over and over again that the flesh is corrupt, and the human heart deceitful and desperately wicked. Indeed about the only thing unregenerated flesh and heart can do is fail. This is not cynicism; it is divine truth.

"But God," continues the Psalmist, "is the strength of my heart." When God touches the heart, something happens to it. Weakness becomes strength, and sin is cleansed. The only way to have that happen to your heart is to acknowledge its natural depravity and ask God to renew it through the blood of Christ. Yes, that is old fashioned doctrine! But it is also the only doctrine that works with sinful hearts.

FEBRUARY 24

The Lord taketh my part (Ps. 118:7).

Every Christian is entitled to say this, but he must be very careful that he does not say it at the wrong time. When there is temptation to be withstood or sorrow to be faced, then the Lord directly takes your part. When you are pushing forward some work for Him against the bitter opposition of the enemy, then indeed God takes your part. But whenever you are acting in self-will or submitting to sin, you must be cautious lest you misapply these precious words. The Lord can never take your part in furthering unhallowed deeds or in consummating tainted desires. Beware of the blasphemy of asking God to help along your sin. Yet there is still a sense in which He takes your part even in your wandering ways. For then He acts in holy resistance of your weak and wicked self-will. And though He may have to bring disciplinary judgment into your life, He is yet working for your ultimate good. "The Lord taketh my part."

FEBRUARY 25

He must increase, but I must decrease (John 3:30).

In this oft-quoted statement of John the Baptist, we see that the exaltation of Christ and the diminution of self are inseparably connected. The grammatical form of the original sentence is enlightening. "He *must* increase," said John, using the imperative word *dei*. The converse statement is elliptical, omitting the imperative.

Surely we need not seek very far for the significance of this construction. It tells us that the imperative thing is always the exaltation of Christ. When He is magnified, self invariably and inevitably decreases. In other words, the end to which our spiritual effort must be directed is the magnifying of Christ. When this is done, our own decreasing is bound to follow. The man who in his own strength strives to humiliate himself runs the danger of false humility. But he whose heart is set only on Christ's increasing will have no trouble with self-inflation.

FEBRUARY 26

He that hath no rule over his own spirit is like a city that is broken down, and without walls (Prov. 25: 28).

Here is a vivid picture of what happens when self masters a man. While not spectacular, self-control is one of the most essential of all the virtues. We Christians ought never to forget that it belongs in the nine-fold fruit of the Spirit enumerated by Paul in Galatians 5:22, 23: "But the fruit of the Spirit is love, joy, peace, longsuffering, kindness, goodness, faithfulness, meekness, self-control" (R.V.).

Lacking self-control, a person is in the very position so graphically described by Solomon under this figure of a ruined city. The walls that hem about the integrity of his personality are broken down; he is open to every assault of the enemy, every attack of the adversary, every temptation of the devil.

Let each of us Christians remember that for him true self-control comes from God-control. Only he who has given Christ full charge over his life has himself best in hand.

FEBRUARY 27

The wind was contrary (Matt. 14:24).

You and I are bound to live many days in the teeth of
contrary winds. As the waves were whipped up on Galilee,
so the tempests will sweep over us. Perhaps this is such a
day for you; perhaps another like it looms in the near
horizon. But just read the rest of this chapter and see how
foolish you are to dread the contrary wind. Remember that,
as the billows mounted on Galilee and the little boat was well
nigh swamped the Lord Jesus "went unto them, walking on
the sea." That storm was memorable to the disciples because
through it Jesus came to them so very wonderfully.

Learn, then, that in your contrary winds Christ may also
come to you. Rejoice in the storm; it may make the Lord
known to you in a new and living way.

FEBRUARY 28

*Wherefore He is able to save them to the uttermost that
come unto God by Him* (Heb. 7: 25).

Can any of us define how far "the uttermost" is? How far
from the earth, for instance, is the uttermost star in the
heavens? Well, if we knew that distance and even if we
could sin to the extent of getting that far away from God,
Christ would still be able to save us. The blessed truth is
simply this, that no one is ever beyond saving, provided that
he comes to God through Christ. And there, in that qualification, lies the only reason why men die in their sins when
redemption is freely offered them. They die in their sins just
because they refuse to "come unto God by Him." Because
they insist upon coming in their own way and thus spurning
God's gift of His Son, they are lost.

It is a solemn thought that a man may come to God
twenty times a day, his whole life may even be a prayer,
he may be moral and devoted, and yet be irrevocably lost
for the one reason that he has not come unto God by Christ
and Christ alone. Are you sure that you have "come unto
God by Him?"

FEBRUARY 29

Finally, brethren, farewell. Be perfect (II Cor. 13:11).

More harm is done Christianity by watering down its standards than by all the misguided Puritanism that ever existed. The whole tendency of our day is to make the Christian life too easy. How often religious people say, as a pallid excuse for their feeble and self-indulgent lives, "But we're only human after all." "Only human," yes. But God holds Christians up to a superhuman standard. Since when is humanity our pattern? "This is My beloved Son," said God, "hear ye Him." "Christ also suffered for us, leaving us an example that ye should follow His steps," said Peter. "Let this mind be in you, which was also in Christ Jesus," said the same Paul, who exhorted the Corinthian believers in our words for today, to "be perfect." And the Lord Jesus Himself gave this command, "Be ye therefore perfect, even as your Father Which is in Heaven is perfect."

But are you and I perfect? Though every one of us must every day answer negatively, still the divine word remains unchanged. "Be perfect." Only as we keep our eyes upon the perfect Christ do we see our utter need of His grace; only as we look to Him are we daily conformed more and more unto His image until the day when that which is in part shall be done away and we shall be like Him, for we shall see Him as He is.

Teach me, O Lord, Thy holy way,
And give me an obedient mind;
That in Thy service I may find
My soul's delight from day to day.

Help me, O Saviour, here to trace
The sacred footsteps Thou hast trod;
And meekly walking with my God,
To grow in goodness, truth, and grace.

MARCH 1

Christ, in Whom are hid all the treasures of wisdom and knowledge (Col. 2: 2, 3).

We need a greater awareness of the hidden riches of our Lord. For Paul to exclaim that "in Him are hid all the treasures of wisdom and knowledge" is sober truth, not mere literary exaggeration. There is a good deal of wisdom and knowledge in the world not directly related to Christ. It may have its place in relation to science or art or many other human activities, but it is not spiritual. The wisdom of Christ differs from human wisdom not only in degree but also in kind. Thus Paul speaks of *"the treasures* of the wisdom and knowledge of Christ." When it comes to these precious things the Lord Jesus is the only repository. Oh, that we might more fully lay hold of the truth that the best is always in Christ!

MARCH 2

A double minded man is unstable in all his ways (James 1:8).

It is perhaps a pity that the translators of our great King James Version did not give us the literal rendering of this striking characterization of an all-too-prevalent type of religious person. "Double minded" is vivid, but the literal "two-souled" is far better—"A two-souled person"! Are you such an one? Is your life divided, so that you are trying with one part of you to live for the Lord, while your other self loves and serves the world?

Psychologists tell us that there is such a thing as the split personality and that it may lead to dire consequences. What those who suffer from it need is to be put together or "integrated," to use the more technical term. And what is true of psychology applies even more to the spiritual life. The Lord Jesus Christ is able to put us together spiritually; He can integrate our souls; He can deliver us from the spiritual instability of being two-souled. For He is the great Physician of sick souls. To experience His healing power we must do one thing: we must place ourselves with complete abandon and entire unreserve in His pierced hands.

MARCH 3

Jesus answered them and said, My doctrine is not Mine, but His that sent Me (John 7:16).

What the Lord Jesus said of His own doctrine we Christians may reverently apply to ourselves. For we know that He has sent us into the world, even as His Father sent Him (John 17:18). Let us always remember, therefore, that the doctrine we teach is not ours but Christ's. Whenever we bear witness to our faith, whether it be in a pulpit, or in personal conversation, in a letter or through the printed page, we can rest upon the fact that the doctrine is not ours but Christ's Who sent us. But we can only have this assurance when we cling close to the doctrine set forth in Scripture. Any departure in preaching or personal witness from the Word of God is a serious thing, because it means nothing less than departure from the doctrine of Christ.

MARCH 4

I love the Lord, because He hath heard my voice and my supplications. Because He hath inclined His ear unto me, therefore will I call upon Him as long as I live (Ps. 116:1, 2).

Have you learned, after bringing your supplications to the Lord in prayer, simply to *rest* in the assurance that He has heard you? After all, how little real trust in Him many of us have. It is all very well for us to *talk* about trusting God. But when we have voiced our supplications to Him and then, after rising from our knees, go right on worrying, we are practicing nothing less than unbelief, whatever our lips may be saying about faith.

Our verse for today expresses very beautifully the inexpressible comfort of knowing that the Lord hears His children. Unlike earthly rulers He is never too busy to hearken to the suppliant. Never is He uninterested in the cries of His dear ones, for His interest in us is as wide as His infinite love. Oh, the wonderful patience of God in just listening to His children! And the marvelous grace of God in acting, with all His infinite power, to fulfill every one of their supplications that is according to His will!

MARCH 5

And as He prayed, the fashion of His countenance was altered, and His raiment was white and glistering (Luke 9:29).

With the Lord Jesus the time of prayer was the time of transfiguration. "As He prayed, the fashion of His countenance was altered." And we too may reverently say that the time of our prayer is the time when we are being changed into His image. In prayer we talk with God; in prayer He makes Himself known to us. In prayer the fashion of our lives are altered, so that daily they approach more and more unto the glory of Christ's life. Would you be like Him? Then seek His face on your knees.

MARCH 6

Every way of a man is right in his own eyes: but the Lord pondereth the hearts (Prov. 21: 2).

The contrast is between man's way of looking at himself and God's way of looking at man. Man is naturally lenient in his view of his own ways. The whole tendency of human thought is to rationalize sin and find an excuse for iniquity. There is no crime too horrible to lack explanation and palliation from somebody. In a sense we are all like Job in our self-justification, although we may fall far short of his righteousness. But God looks at us differently. He not only sees our ways; He sees clear through them down into the hidden motives of the heart that brings them forth. His vision is not a fleeting one. As He sees, He ponders. The Almighty balances motive against motive, feeling against feeling. He judges and evaluates our most secret thoughts. Who of us can doubt His verdict? With impartial justice He must declare, not of one man but of all, "There is none righteous, no, not one" (Rom. 3:11).

But God does not stop with condemnation. He Who ponders our hearts, ponders also our need. And so He has given His Son to be the substitute for us who are unrighteous. He has pondered our lost condition with the result that His infinite love has brought forth the plan of salvation. And He is still pondering our hearts to do us good and to meet our "every need according to His riches in glory by Christ Jesus" (Phil. 4:19).

MARCH 7

I poured out my complaint before Him; I showed before Him my trouble (Ps. 142:2).

There is a therapeutic value in unburdening the soul. Troubles are eased just by the telling of them. But to what man or woman, however closely united to us, do we either dare or desire to tell *all* of our troubles? In most of our lives there are things that we can bring to no human ear, for we are not sure that we shall be understood. Yet how we long to unburden ourselves! What an unspeakable comfort it is, then, to know that we can say anything to God. No secret is too dark for Him to illumine; no fear is too formidable for Him to dispel; no problem is too difficult for Him to solve. Oh, if we believers would only do like the psalmist and pour out our complaints before God.

MARCH 8

And they were afraid (Mark 5:15).

What these Gadarenes were afraid of is significant. They happened to have in their community a man who, being possessed of evil spirits, had fallen to the level of a wild beast. But when he came into contact with the Lord Jesus, he was healed; for Jesus had cast the demons into a herd of swine which rushed headlong into the sea. And then we read of the fear of the Gadarenes. Hearing of the loss of their swine, "they come to Jesus, and see him who was possessed with the demon, and had the legion, sitting, and clothed, and in his right mind: *and they were afraid.*" Afraid of what? Of the man clothed and in his right mind! That is what the selfishness of sin does; it warps judgment to such a degree that spiritual peace and health actually give rise to fear.

There are many today who are like those ancient Gadarenes. Sin has twisted our scale of values until we are afraid of the godly sanity Christ alone can give. Something very drastic happens when a man is born again. Among other things his whole life-outlook is re-oriented. What seems sensible to the world is folly to him: what is folly to him is wisdom to the world. Christ's mind is the only completely sane and balanced mind. Oh, let us accept it gladly and without fear!

MARCH 9

Now to Him that is of power . . . (Rom. 16: 25).

This introduction to the great doxology with which Paul
closes the chief of his epistles might well preface our daily
prayer and worship. The God to Whom we look is a God
of power. He is an able God, "able to do exceeding abundantly above all that we ask or think." Whatever else may
be true of our petitions, there is one premise that never can
be shaken. God does have the power to answer our prayers
because nothing is too hard for Him. The God Whom we
praise and glorify and to Whom we bring the desires of our
hearts is the God of power, power infinite, universal, eternal.
It is therefore no light matter to petition His aid. For when
He helps nothing can thwart His purpose.

MARCH 10

For the vision is yet for an appointed time, but at the
end it shall speak, and not lie; though it tarry, wait for it;
because it will surely come, it will not tarry (Hab. 2: 3).

Habakkuk's time was much like our own. He saw goodness outraged, the weak oppressed, cruelty rampant. His
soul was stirred within him and he cried out to God against
the flagrant injustices of the aggressor. And then Habakkuk
went alone to his watchtower. As he spread the matter before
the Lord, the answer came, introduced by our text for today.
The vision, the fulfillment of justice, says God, is for an
appointed time. Though it seem to the prophet to tarry, he
is to wait for it; it will surely come, it will not tarry. In other
words, from man's point of view the vision is tardy of fulfillment, but from God's point of view it is precisely timed.
"It will surely come, it will not tarry."

Oh, the comfort of knowing that our God is never late! We
may long for His intervention; we may even accuse Him,
as did Habakkuk, of letting evil flourish unrebuked. Nevertheless, His hand is never tardy. At the appointed time He
intervenes. His time is, out of all eternity, the one perfect
time for action. So let us put aside anxiety. God will not be
late in keeping His appointments for mercy and judgment.

MARCH 11

And he, casting away his garment, rose, and came to Jesus (Mark 10:50).

Let us notice this action of blind Bartimaeus. The garment mentioned was undoubtedly a long cloak, as might have hampered his activity. But Christ called Bartimaeus, and without a moment's hesitation he threw aside the thing that could delay his response. Oh, that we might be like-minded when our Lord speaks to us! He calls to us to do a task, to serve Him in some special way. But what garments impede us—the impressive robe of pride, the costly cloak of worldly possessions, the defiled gown of sinful indulgence! When the Lord Jesus speaks to us, there is one thing only to be done with such things; they *must* be cast aside.

MARCH 12

And when they came to Marah, they could not drink of the waters of Marah, for they were bitter (Exod. 15: 23).

As you read further in this chapter, you will see that God directed Moses to cast a tree into the bitter waters, whereby they were sweetened, so that the thirsty people could drink. Now there are several things we may learn from this incident of long ago. In the first place, the bitter waters of Marah were directly in the path of God's people, and God Himself was leading them. So in our own pilgrimages there come the Marah experiences—times of drastic testing and overwhelming difficulty. Yet we continue to sing in faith, "He leadeth me." And it *is* true; God does lead us, even to the bitter waters of Marah. But that is not all. He who brings us to those waters provides the tree to sweeten them, even the Cross of our Lord Jesus Christ.

Perhaps you are this day at some Marah in your life. Then may you learn the blessed truth of the Cross as applied to you and as Paul knew it when he cried out, "I am crucified with Christ." No child of God need ever doubt his Lord's faithfulness in sanctifying to him his deepest distress.

MARCH 13

If ye abide in Me, and My words abide in you, ye shall ask what ye will, and it shall be done unto you (John 15:7).

In interpreting Scripture much depends upon which words are stressed. Here is a case in point. No Christian has a right to emphasize the last clause of this glorious verse at the expense of the first one. For the Lord Jesus did not just say, "You shall ask what ye will, and it shall be done unto you." He prefaced these great words with a condition, and no interpretation of the verse is valid which slights that little introductory *if*, followed by its conditional clause.

And what is that condition? It is to abide in Christ and to have His words abiding in us. So we find abiding to be the key to prayer. For those who truly abide in Christ, those who have His words deep in their souls, will, out of that union with Him, offer prayers that are in accord with the divine will.

MARCH 14

Quicken us, and we will call upon Thy Name (Ps. 80:18).

Consider this ancient prayer of Asaph. It is really a prayer for revival. There are many Christians who are similarly calling upon God for quickening. But it is the second clause, which is the sequel to the prayer, that speaks especially to us. "Quicken us, revive us," cried Asaph, "but do it so that we may call upon Thy Name." Surely that is the gist of his words. And the thought is worth our pondering.

Is there not nowadays a great deal of futile praying for revival—praying that is useless, because of its ultimate purpose? Can God send revival to Christian workers who chiefly want the glory of participating in a big spiritual movement? Will He quicken those who are mostly interested in the spiritual aggrandizement of reputation that will be theirs? Those are serious questions. But when a soul cries out, like Asaph, "Quicken us, and we will call upon Thy Name"; when a soul seeks new spiritual life for spiritual ends only, that is something quite different. Let us pray for quickening, but let us pray for it with a spiritual purpose.

MARCH 15

Face to face (III John 14).

John uses the phrase at the close of this letter, as he speaks of seeing his friend Gaius shortly. Surely Gaius must have looked forward to that meeting with the beloved disciple. An infinitely greater meeting awaits us. Some day we shall see our Lord face to face. And when we do behold Him we shall be transformed; "we shall be like Him, for we shall see Him as He is." Every Christian has a letter from his Lord promising that meeting. That letter is the New Testament, and it tells us that Jesus is coming and that He is coming soon.

MARCH 16

Pure religion and undefiled before God and the Father is this, To visit the fatherless and widows in their affliction, and to keep himself unspotted from the world (James 1: 27).

It is somewhat surprising that the word "religion" is used but three times in all the Bible—twice in this chapter of James and once in Acts 26:5. The word is in no sense synonymous with salvation, but rather means external worship. Thus in our verse for today James is describing the outward manifestation of the faith of the heart. What he is saying is that the purest worship of God lies not in religious rites and ceremonies but in two things—service to the afflicted and separation from worldly contamination. The first is outward in that it affects others; the second is inward in that it relates to the individual life.

What kind of religion do you have, measured by James's test? And when you have so examined yourself, remember that there is always opportunity to help the afflicted; they are ever present. Moreover, there is always the need to be unspotted from the world, for the world will never be anything but contaminating. May the religion of every Christian who reads these words be pure and undefiled this day!

MARCH 17

Cleanse Thou me from secret faults (Ps. 19:12).

Our thought for today is a very simple one—just the emphasis of one word in this brief prayer of David. Read it this way: "Cleanse Thou *me* from secret faults." Take your pencil and encircle that third word. Oh, we need to pray less about other people's sins and more about our own! We need to ask the Lord to deal with *our* secret faults, of which there are many. For only when we see our sins do we begin to realize the riches of saving grace. Unless we have learned to read our Bibles in this personal way, we have yet to enter in upon the transforming power it can exert over our lives. But let us not dare to pray to God, "Cleanse Thou *me* from secret faults," unless we are willing to have Him obliterate even our most hidden and darling sins.

MARCH 18

Sorrow is better than laughter (Eccles. 7:3).

Before dismissing this word of Solomon as a counsel of pessimism let us think about it for a moment. What a person laughs at tells much about his character. The trouble with the world today is that the wrong things amuse it. Much that is holy gives rise to flippancy; much that is tragic becomes a joke. However man looks at them there are some things that in God's sight are never funny. And when the world is amused at spirituality, jokes about redemption, and laughs at sin, it is an offense to a Holy God, no matter how clever it may be.

Ah, yes, Christian, be happy. Cherish your sense of humor. But remember that when your Lord said, "Blessed are they that mourn, for they shall be comforted," He was referring not only to the bereaved but also to those who are mourning because of their sin. For the joy of forgiveness comes only after the sorrow of penitence. If you have never really mourned for your sin, you have yet to know what Christian happiness means.

MARCH 19

If Balak would give me his house full of silver and gold, I cannot go beyond the word of the Lord my God, to do less or more. Now therefore, I pray you, tarry ye also here this night, that I may know what the Lord will say unto me more (Num. 22:18, 19).

Those were noble words that Balaam spoke to the deputation sent him by Balak. But how sad is their immediate sequel. For Balaam fell into his old error of giving house room to the tempters. It sounded very pious for him to say that he would ask God about their wicked proposal, but he had no right to go to God again with that same matter, for God had clearly forbidden him to have anything to do with it (vs. 12).

Balaam is a type of the deceitfulness of the human heart. We know the right, we know that sin is sin, yet like Balaam we play with it. We think that God will let us be on friendly terms with some evil. We even pray about things that we know are against His holy will. Oh, that we might learn that, when God says "No" to us on any moral or spiritual issue, He means "No" eternally and irrevocably!

MARCH 20

And Moses brought their cause before the Lord (Num. 27:5).

Moses is indeed a refreshing contrast to the compromising Balaam. Few of us remember the exact details of his perplexity in the instance of the daughters of Zelophehad. But what a magnificent example Moses set in his dealing with it. He took his problem to God for settlement. He "brought their cause before the Lord." And then, having received the answer, Moses did what God commanded.

May we see him today as a type of Christ our High Priest and Advocate. We have our perplexities. Not one of us but has some problem too hard for him. Let us bring the difficulty to Christ Who perfectly represents us before the Father. With Him are hid all the treasures of knowledge. He will solve our hardest problems and bear our heaviest burdens.

MARCH 21

And they were both righteous before God (Luke 1: 6).

There is all the difference in the world between righteousness before men and righteousness before God. Sometimes a Christian is placed in the position of maintaining righteousness before God at the cost of losing righteousness before men. And sometimes righteousness before men exacts the price of loss of righteousness in the divine eyes. The world judges harshly those who do not conform to its standards and who are not righteous in its sight. But the world's view of righteousness is distorted. Trust in Christ for your righteousness, follow His will as He reveals it through His Word, and do not be concerned at the world's opinion. That is the way of Christian integrity.

MARCH 22

The Son of God, Who loved me, and gave Himself for me (Gal. 2: 20).

"For me." In those two words lies the heart of Paul's spiritual experience. He had an intensely individual hold upon Christ; the Saviour of the world was preëminently his own Saviour, Who had died for him as an individual. Have you ever reflected upon this matter of personal relationship? Think how highly personal contact with the world's great is valued. Very few of us are so impervious to earthly prestige as not to consider personal acquaintance with great men and women an outstanding privilege. But how immeasurably greater is our privilege as Christians of intimate relationship with the Lord Jesus. Paul's spiritual experience was uniquely his. Christ died for him as an individual. But have you grasped the amazing fact that you may be just as individually related to Christ as was Paul? He Who died for the Apostle died for you. As Paul says in II Corinthians, "He died for all." He is your Saviour. He will be exactly as close to you as you will come close to Him. Were we to value His personal friendship more, surely we should take more time in cultivating it.

MARCH 23

All these things did Araunah, as a king, give unto the king (II Sam. 24: 23).

You may not be a king, but it is possible for you to act as a king. Take a lesson from Araunah, who had a threshing-floor that King David desired. The commoner rose to kingly stature, for what he had he freely placed at David's disposal with a truly royal gesture. So may you do with everything you have and are. Because every believer is the Lord's servant, the Lord Jesus sees something in you that He needs. Then do as Araunah and give it to Him "as a king." There is no joy greater than that of giving truly to the Lord.

MARCH 24

I acknowledged my sin unto Thee, and mine iniquity have I not hid. I said, I will confess my transgressions unto the Lord; and Thou forgavest the iniquity of my sin. Selah (Ps. 32: 5).

The word "Selah," meaning a pause for meditation, is well placed after this verse, in which David shows how a man who has formerly missed the blessing of transgression forgiven and sin covered may yet experience that blessedness. The way into the primary beatitude is simply confession. When guile goes and sin is acknowledged, forgiveness comes. But let us not fail to notice two significant phrases—"unto Thee" and "unto the Lord." David is not talking about confession to man, but to God. In the deeper sense of forgiving transgression and covering sin, it is only God Who can act with complete efficacy. Nor is it ever a light matter to confess sin unto God. Confession of our sin unto the Lord is more than a form of penitential words. It is seeing, insofar as we are able, the sin as God sees it; it is looking at the unholy thing with something of the abhorrence of the Holy One; it is acknowledging our own iniquity for which we alone are to blame; it is realizing that the thing we have done is a direct affront not just to a human beloved, not to an exalted ruler of this earth, but to our blessed Lord Who died that we might not do the very sin we have done. Oh, let us beware of thoughtless confession!

MARCH 25

Command the children of Israel, that they bring unto thee pure oil olive beaten for the light, to cause the lamps to burn continually (Lev. 24: 2).

The lamp is the symbol of testimony, just as the oil stands for the Holy Spirit. For the ancient sanctuary God commanded that the lamps be replenished with pure oil. Thus it is with your testimony for Christ. It must be nourished with the oil of the Holy Spirit, which means that the channel of its flow—your life—must be kept clean. "Let your light . . . shine before men," said the Lord Jesus. It is within your power to do that. You provide neither the oil nor the flame. Your part is simply to keep the way clear for the Spirit to flow through you. But in that you have committed to you the shining of your light for Christ.

MARCH 26

For by thy words thou shalt be justified, and by thy words thou shalt be condemned (Matt. 12: 37).

Here is a sentence, the searching implications of which are missed by all too many Christians. It might be summed up thus: "Words are deeds." For in the passage which this verse climaxes, Christ is teaching the abiding reality of words. So real are they, He points out (12:36) that in the day of judgment we are to be held accountable for every idle word. And finally, He continues, the mode of our justification is verbal.

How profound this teaching is! Reflect upon it and you will see the crucial importance of words. How do men and women reject Christ and His salvation? Is it not by some form of words, some expression of the rebellious heart? Nor are all words necessarily spoken. There are the silent words of the heart, the words of the thought-life, multitudes of them idle, others corrupt, others flatly rejecting the Lord Jesus. Yes, words *are* the mode of justification, for with them man either denies his Lord or confesses Him.

What of our words, spoken and unspoken? Will they justify us or condemn us in that inevitable day of accounting before the all-seeing Judge?

MARCH 27

The joy of the Lord is your strength (Neh. 8:10).

God cannot be dissociated from joy. He is light and in Him is no darkness at all. Gloom has nothing to do with Deity, and those who serve Christ without joy are in that respect failing to represent Him truly. Moreover, as Nehemiah puts it in this superb sentence, strength comes from the joy of the Lord. There is nothing trivial about the Lord's joy. It is powerful, and it fortifies the heart in deepest distress.

Take your Bible, trace the theme joy throughout its pages, and you will see that there is no circumstance in which it is inappropriate to rejoice in the Lord. One of the unique elements of the Christian faith is its independence of earthly circumstances. In tribulation and in sorrow, in sickness and in peril, it is possible for you to rejoice. No matter, therefore, what faces you today, you may find strength in the joy of the Lord. "The joy of the Lord *is* your strength."

MARCH 28

Philip findeth Nathanael, and saith unto him, We have found Him, of Whom Moses in the law, and the prophets, did write, Jesus of Nazareth, the son of Joseph (John 1:45).

"We have found Him." The antecedents of these words of Nathanael are especially significant. Philip could indeed say, "We have found Him," but he could only say that because he had first of all been found by Christ. For the second verse back tells us, "The day following Jesus would go forth unto Galilee, and findeth Philip, and saith unto him, Follow Me" (vs. 43). So it is with all of us. We say that we have found the Lord, and, if we are Christians, we have indeed done so. But let us never forget that He has first found us. Each of us is the lost sheep. And if the Lord Jesus had never sought us, even to the extent of laying aside His divine glory in Heaven and coming to earth as a man, we should never, never have found Him Who is our Saviour and our God.

MARCH 29

Set your affection on things above, not on things on the earth. For ye are dead, and your life is hid with Christ in God (Col. 3: 2, 3).

The great principles of the Christian life are not unreasonable. God makes no demands upon His children that are incompatible with the highest spiritual logic. "Set your affection on things above, not on things on the earth," urges the inspired apostle. But he does not stop there. "For," he continues, "ye are dead, and your life is hid with Christ in God." And so, reminding us that in Christ we have died to the former sinful life, he exhorts us with complete reasonableness to set our hearts upon heavenly things. In the light of this, can there be anything more illogical from the spiritual point of view than for us Christians to be clinging in heart to anything at all in that old life to which, in Christ, we have already died?

MARCH 30

And there came of all people to hear the wisdom of Solomon, from all kings of the earth, which had heard of his wisdom (I Kings 4: 34).

Nothing is more attractive than true wisdom. In the case of Solomon, it brought pilgrims from the ends of the earth. But a greater than Solomon has come. And the wisdom which was imparted to Solomon is His by nature and in all its fulness. To Him also there have come and are still coming people from all the kings of the earth.

Notice, however, that it was not "all people" who came to Solomon, but "of all people." There's a difference. Not every one in the wise king's day sought him out; not every one seeks Christ. Yes, Christ is wonderfully attractive, but it is possible to resist His attractiveness. In Him truly "are hid all the treasures of wisdom and knowledge," but men will insist upon consulting their own darkened minds rather than Him Who gave even Solomon his wisdom. In our Lord we believers have wisdom sufficient for every problem that can possibly arise but we must abide in Him if we are to benefit by His knowledge.

MARCH 31

Now faith is the substance of things hoped for, the evidence of things not seen (Heb. 11:1).

Very many of us make the mistake of confusing faith with desire or longing. We look to God for something with real yearning, and we are inclined to call that emotion faith. But it is nothing of the kind. Faith is more than desire, no matter how intense the desire may be. Faith must first and foremost have in it the element of assurance. A more literal translation of our familiar text makes this clear. "Faith," says the original Greek, "is the substantiating (Weymouth translates this word by 'confident assurance') of things hoped for, a conviction of things not seen." In other words, faith not only desires intensely; it actually is convinced of the reality of the unseen object of its desire and its confident assurance works to substantiate that which is as yet only hoped for. And note that this is exactly the teaching of the Lord Jesus when He said to His disciples, "What things soever ye desire, when ye pray, believe that ye receive them, and ye shall have them" (Mark 11: 24).

It is not until we come to the point of really building upon the sure anticipation of something for which we have humbly and prayerfully asked God that we step out from desire into faith. "Oh," someone says, "what presumption to go so far as to count in advance upon the sure answer to our prayer!" Well, it would be presumption indeed but for this: We have a God Who can do anything and Who is faithful to His Word. His Word expresses His will. His Son told us to have faith in Him and then to believe that God will hear us. And when we thus pray on the basis of God's pledged Word, we are praying according to His will. To believe, therefore, that God will do what He has said He will do is not presumption; it is faith in our Heavenly Father's integrity.

> *Faith, mighty faith, the promise sees,*
> *And looks to God alone;*
> *Laughs at impossibilities*
> *And cries, It shall be done!*

APRIL 1

As thou hast believed, so be it done unto thee (Matt. 8:13).

"And his servant was healed in the self-same hour." So concludes the record of this unique incident in our Lord's early ministry. The centurion had come to Christ and he had come with such a faith as to cause the Lord to marvel. In these words Christ states the great spiritual principle that God's power is released by faith. What moves God to act for man is not zealous works of righteousness, not just clamorous petitioning, but simple faith. In and through our good works and in and through our prayers, God is looking for one essential quality—genuine belief in Him. Have you a burden to be lifted, a mountain to be removed? The words of the Lord Jesus to the centurion apply to you today, "As thou hast believed, so be it done unto thee."

APRIL 2

How precious also are Thy thoughts unto me, O God! How great is the sum of them! If I should count them, they are more in number than the sand (Ps. 139:17, 18).

Contrast our loving Father's thoughts of you with the number of your thoughts toward Him, and you will see a precious demonstration of His grace. What a striking figure the psalmist uses of God's multitudinous thoughts for His dear children—"more in number than the sand"! And who has ever counted the grains of sand, even on one square yard of beach? By comparison how utterly meagre are the thoughts you and I have for God.

Let us be very personal about this matter. How many times do you recall thinking of God yesterday? Five times, ten times, fifty times? But what if it were a hundred or a thousand times? How infinitely greater is your heavenly Father's thought of you! He Who numbers the hairs of your head has you constantly in His mind. And so we have one of the ultimate proofs of His true love for us sinful creatures. For true love does not depend upon requital. It keeps right on, even though it is never fully reciprocated. Thus it is with God; infinitely He loves us, finitely and inadequately we requite His love, yet infinitely His love continues in its divinely prodigal thoughtfulness.

APRIL 3

I ascend unto My Father, and your Father; and to My God, and your God (John 20:17).

Marvelously comforting are these words which the Lord Jesus spoke to Mary Magdalene, when He appeared to her so soon after His resurrection. Consider the linking of the pronoun: *"My* Father, and *your* Father . . . *My* God, and *your* God."* What can it mean but that the very same Father God Who had power to vanquish death and bring His dear Son to life was Mary's Father and Mary's God. You have your problems; things are not easy these days; you are well nigh overwhelmed with difficulties. But Christian, what a God you have! He is the same Father, the same God Who raised up Christ. And if it was not too hard for Him to break the sealed tomb and bring life and immortality to light, can you doubt His ability to solve your problems and bring you through your difficulty?

APRIL 4

Nevertheless for David's sake did the Lord his God give him [Abijam] a lamp in Jerusalem . . . because David did that which was right in the eyes of the Lord (I Kings 15:4, 5).

It is worth while to do the will of God, not for your sake alone, but for the sake of others. Scripture records not only the carry-over of evil, but also the carry-over of good. It is true that the sins of the fathers are visited upon the children unto the third and fourth generation. And it is also true that good does not die with the doer, but carries over to bless the posterity. The principle of representation is at the very foundation of God's government. Adam represented us, and in him we all died. But in Christ we shall all be made alive. So in our smaller sphere each of us acts for others. And when this solemn truth lays hold upon a person, he dare not consciously do evil. For those who love their fellowman, next to what sin does to the heart of God, the greatest deterrent from evil is the thought of what it will do not to one's self but to others. Would that more of us were living so that God could bless *many* for our sakes!

APRIL 5

And Elijah said unto her, Fear not; go and do as thou hast said: but make me thereof a little cake first, and bring it unto me, and after make for thee and for thy son (I Kings 17:13).

Let us learn today from the widow of Zarephath. As she was preparing her last meal before her death and that of her son in the famine, the prophet met her. But because she obeyed the voice of God through Elijah she lived. What then did Elijah tell her that she might live and not die? Just two things: 1. In the face of imminent death to give up fear; 2. To take care of God's part first, despite her own extremity. And because the widow did these two things (vs. 15), "she, and he, and her house, did eat many days."

These two simple steps have never been superseded. The door to God's perfect supply of our need is still entered through refusing to fear and through giving the first place, despite our most pressing personal need, to what God asks us to do for Him.

APRIL 6

Having made known unto us the secret of His will (Eph. 1: 9, Young's Literal Translation).

"The secret of His will." Is it not wonderful to think that the only wise God has chosen to take us into His confidence to the extent of revealing to us "the secret of His will"? Imagine that your President or King calls you personally to him for the purpose of taking you into His confidence as to some cherished plans. Would you not be insulting, were you disinterested and unwilling even to hear what he has to tell you? Yet God has spoken to men in His Holy Word. And in portions of that Word He has actually "made known the secrets of His will." But men are disinterested. They just do not care about the things the Ruler of the Universe has to tell them.

Here lies the sin in the Christian's failure to read and study the Bible. That the unbeliever has no heart for God's revelation may be understandable. But that God should make known His will even to the extent of showing forth His secret counsels, and that the believer should just not care about inquiring into the mysteries of that divine will—that is unthinkable. Yes, neglect of our Bible is sin.

APRIL 7

Lord, teach us to pray (Luke 11:1)

Let us think again about this verse, particularly the first word, for that is its key. *"Lord,"* cried the disciples, "teach us to pray." If you and I ever learn to pray, it will be only because Christ has taught us. If we ever learn to pray, it will be because we acknowledge Him as the Lord of the inner chamber as well as of the external life. If we ever learn to pray, it will be only when, as Dr. Andrew Murray said, we come to the place of confessing to the Lord Jesus our total inability to pray of ourselves. Real prayer, powerful, prevailing prayer, is a thoroughly supernatural thing. It can no more grow out of the soil of our sinful, natural lives than a rose can grow out of solid granite. But the Lord Jesus can give us the gift and power of prayer through our new regenerate nature. Oh, let us turn to Him alone as our prayer Teacher.

APRIL 8

What confidence is this wherein thou trustest? (II Kings 18:19).

In the fourteenth year of his reign Hezekiah faced a powerful invader in the person of Sennacherib, King of Assyria. Just as the aggressor of our day attempts to overawe his victims with threats of violence, so Rab-shakeh, the Assyrian emissary, insolently challenged the godly Hezekiah. His words, so extensively reported in this chapter, contain this question: "What confidence is this in which thou trustest?"

It is a good question for us; it was a good question for Hezekiah, even though it came from the lips of a Rab-shakeh and was uttered to strike fear into the king's heart. But it failed of its purpose. For Hezekiah, asking himself wherein he was trusting, was simply driven back upon the Lord and thus strengthened immeasurably.

How about you? Not to be terrified but to be helped, ask yourself, "What confidence is this wherein I am trusting?" If your answer is "Christ," no modern Rab-shakeh, be he the ambassador of the Evil One himself, can daunt you.

APRIL 9

And whatsoever we ask, we receive of Him, because we keep His commandments, and do those things that are pleasing in His sight (I John 3: 22).

Although the word "if" is not used, this verse nevertheless sets forth an important condition of answered prayer. John says that Christians who keep God's commandments and do the things that are pleasing to Him (i.e., do His will) receive whatsoever they ask. "We receive . . . because we keep His commandments, and do His will." That is the principle.

Obviously, therefore, one of the keys to answered prayer is obedience. And John is very explicit in defining the kind of obedience God requires as a preliminary to answered prayer. For the next verse explains the two-fold nature of the commandment we are to keep. "This is His commandment, that we should believe on the Name of His Son Jesus Christ, and love one another, as He gave us commandment." In the light of this passage we simply have to make certain that our daily prayers are issuing from hearts that are truly loving and believing.

APRIL 10

And again He entered into Capernaum after some days; and it was noised that He was in the house. And straightway many were gathered together, insomuch that there was no room to receive them, no, not so much as about the door (Mark 2:1, 2).

This vivid report of one of Christ's visits to Capernaum shows us His wonderful attractiveness. The news of His arrival meant an immediate crowd. So today Christ is still attractive to men, as He is manifest in the lives of His devoted disciples. The believer who is really yielded to the Lord Jesus is a winsome person. It is extremely doubtful whether a repellent personality can be consistent with holy living. Austerity may indeed be forbidding, but austerity is not Christ-likeness. We believers are all that many a worldling will see of our blessed Lord. May we therefore be so surrendered to His indwelling Presence that His own wonderful attractiveness shall be clearly seen in us! Our prayer should be that of the old chorus, "Let the Beauty of Jesus be seen in Me."

APRIL 11

Then said Hezekiah unto Isaiah, Good is the Word of the Lord which Thou hast spoken (II Kings 20:19).

To appreciate the greatness of this reply we must go back to what the king had just heard from the lips of Isaiah: "Hear the Word of the Lord. Behold the days come, that all that is in thine house . . . shall be carried into Babylon: nothing shall be left, saith the Lord" (vss. 16, 17). Hezekiah was a great man, but he never was greater than when, having sinned through pride, he heard these words and said to the prophet, "Good is the Word of the Lord which thou hast spoken."

There come times for all of us when God has to chastise us. Oh, may we then be of the moral stature of Hezekiah! May we be like him in uttering not one word of complaint, but in simply receiving the judgment with the humble acknowledgment, "Good is the Word of the Lord; good are the things which the Lord has done."

APRIL 12

I shall not die but live, and declare the works of the Lord (Ps. 118:17).

What is your purpose in life? For the psalmist it was the exalted purpose of declaring the works of the Lord. Like Paul he reckoned himself as one who was alive from the dead, and he meant his life to count in the highest service. Can you as a Christian who has been brought to life from death in trespasses and sins afford to have a lower purpose than declaring the mighty works of your Saviour-God? After all, there is but one proper vocation for redeemed souls, and that is the proclamation of the Gospel.

Oh yes, we may be making our living in business or in a profession. Those things are all very well as a means of livelihood, but behind them lies our vocation under God. And that is nothing less than to declare His saving work for sinners. We do not need a church nor a sermon to follow that vocation. Our office or home may be our church and our consistent Christian life our sermon. Are we following the lofty vocation to which God has called us?

APRIL 13

Them that honour Me I will honour (I Sam. 2: 30).

This is not only a word of encouragement to all faithful believers; it is also a divine pledge that God will not fail to keep. But like other heavenly promises, it must be viewed in the light of eternity. The coming day of unveiling will reveal things hidden in this temporal life. Then will be seen what shall be done to those whom the King delighteth to honor. Meanwhile our concern is not with how and when God will keep His promise. Our concern is whether or not we really are honoring Him.

Are you reading these words in the morning? Then examine your plans for the day and resolutely put away any of them that cannot be followed to the honor of God. Or perhaps you are reading this in the evening. Then look back, ask forgiveness for what you did that was not honoring to the Lord, and resolve with His help to eschew it on the morrow.

APRIL 14

Except the Lord build the house, they labour in vain that build it: except the Lord keep the city, the watchman waketh but in vain (Ps. 127:1).

This is the psalmist's poetical way of stating the very practical principle that anything we undertake is futile unless the Lord be given primacy in it. The Christian life is a partnership. In a business the junior partner is guided by his senior's advice; he does not begin new projects on his own initiative. But we Christians are prone to act quite differently. How easy it is for us to plan things without really consulting God! We are all too ready in personal and family affairs and in business ventures to go ahead without first seeking God's counsel. We build the house according to our own specifications and watch the city on our own schedule, and things go wrong. To be sure, disaster does not always follow immediately upon such a course of action, but there is one thing that does happen in every case: blessing is lost.

APRIL 15

For He received from God the Father honour and glory . . .
(II Peter 1:17).

This is part of Peter's own recollection of our Lord's transfiguration. May it lead us to ask ourselves the question
whether Christ has received from us that which God the
Father gave Him on the holy mount nineteen hundred years
ago. Can it be, after all, that we are relegating Him to a
place in our little lives that is secondary to the things of
the world? God has decreed that Christ should have nothing
less than the supreme honor and glory. We may not have
riches or fame to give our Saviour, but every one of us can
let Him have honor and glory in our lives.

APRIL 16

A good name is rather to be chosen than great riches
(Prov. 22:1).

Let us meditate upon the priceless possession of a name
highly esteemed. Solomon sets such a name above great
riches. The contrast is significant. Men toil for riches. And
let no one deny that to amass great wealth takes devotion
to purpose and hard, hard work. But the work is directed
to one end and that end is so often a selfish one that the
pursuit of riches frequently ruins the name.

Not so the good name. It is a by-product, not an end in
itself. So with the Christian life. It was the risen Lord Jesus,
as John records His words in the message to the church at
Pergamos (Rev. 2:17) Who said, "To him that overcometh
. . . will I give a white stone, and in the stone a new name
written." Though that name is a mystery, still we know this
about it; it is "a good name" and "rather to be chosen than
great riches."

APRIL 17

With my soul have I desired Thee in the night (Isa. 26:9).

Have you ever had a sleepless night? Then you know how distressing those wakeful hours may be. But, though sleep be denied, you may nevertheless receive the compensation of soul-strengthening blessing by doing what Isaiah describes in these words: "With my soul I sought Him in the night." For when you seek your Lord thus, He will not be far from you. And in the quiet of the night it is your privilege to have uninterrupted and prolonged fellowship with Him which the busy day simply does not permit. Our Lord Who knew what it was to linger all night in prayer has some precious things to say to those who seek Him in their wakeful hours.

APRIL 18

Blessed are all they that put their trust in Him (Ps. 2:12).

The second Psalm is such a marvelous condensation of Messianic prophecy that the beatitude with which it closes may have been neglected by many readers. Yet of all the Scripture beatitudes none is more comforting than this one. "Blessed are *all* they that put their trust in Him." What a wealth of assurance lies in that word "all"! It states a great principle of the spiritual life—that trusting is the sure prelude to blessing. It shows that there are no exceptions in God's faithfulness. Look trustingly to the Lord and you *will* be blessed. The sequence is rooted in the divine logic. And that wonderful word "all" transcends time and outward circumstance. "All," both now and in the past and in the future, "all" who possess the single qualification of putting their trust in God, will be blessed.

Let us, however, be careful to avoid a low view of the qualifying clause in the beatitude. Christians who really know what it means to put their trust in the Lord are all too uncommon. For trusting God, which is the precursor of blessedness, means committal of everything to Him.

APRIL 19

God is faithful (I Cor. 1: 9).

Yes, we know that God is faithful, but what a comfort it is just to be reminded of the blessed fact. Let friends fail and relatives forsake us, our God is faithful. But to what is He faithful? Two words give the answer—His promises. Therefore, if we would really appreciate His faithfulness, we must first know His promises. There is no surer way to grow spiritually than to search the Word for God's promises, to rest upon them when you have found them, and then to praise Him for His faithfulness to them. A promise a day, treasured in the heart and really believed, will give you a grip on God's faithfulness that you will never lose.

APRIL 20

They knew Him, and ran . . . (Mark 6: 54, 55).

They ran, Mark goes on to explain, for a very particular purpose—"to carry about in beds those that were sick" and to lay "the sick in the streets," beseeching Him "that they might touch if it were but the border of His garment." That was indeed wonderful, and many were healed and blessed through the efforts of those who so purposefully and help-fully ran. But let us get back to the cause. "They knew Him," says Mark. When the Lord Jesus landed at Gennesaret, the people recognized Him. And having recognized Him they could not wait, but just had to run to put the sick in touch with His healing power.

Is it not all a parable of Christian life and service today? You and I, dear believer, are like the people of Gennesaret in that we have seen and known Christ. But are we sufficiently like them to do what they did in hastening to bring the needy to Him? Have you, since your conversion, ever been in a hurry to bring the Gospel to anyone? Oh, the sad reluctance of our witnessing! How slow we are when it comes to lead-ing souls to Christ. "They knew Him, and ran." Our busi-ness is urgent. Let us not waste precious time in setting about it.

APRIL 21

I know that Thou canst do everything (Job 42:2).

When a man or woman comes to that attitude in relation to God, then all his problems are settled. When one really acknowledges, as did Job, the absolute supremacy of God, his agonized questionings of his sore affliction are ended. The problem of permitted evil finds its solution not in logic or philosophy, but in the greatness of God. A humble acknowledgment of His majestic sovereignty brings peace amid the direst trouble. The question is not whether you can reconcile predestination and free will, whether you can "justify the ways of God to man" in their entirety. The question is just this: How great a God have you? If your faith envisions the greatness of Job's God, your affliction will issue in the peace that came to Job.

APRIL 22

Let us hear the conclusion of the whole matter: Fear God, and keep His commandments: for this is the whole duty of man (Eccles. 12:13).

The conclusion of the Preacher is true, but how shallow in their thinking are those who would build upon it an ethical religion of salvation by works. For, rightly considered, these words are among the most stringently demanding in all the Bible. What does God require of man? Just two things, the moralist replies: To fear Him and to keep His commandments. Yes, just two things, but who ever does them? Who of all the sons and daughters of men really fears God as He ought to be feared? Who keeps *all* of His holy commandments? The truth of the matter is that these apparently simple requirements expand, as we prayerfully reflect upon them, into demands far beyond the power of sinful men to meet. So the just and true law of God becomes our schoolmaster to lead us to Christ and His salvation by grace. Just because we do not fear God as we ought—just because we continually break His commandments—we need imputed to us through faith the perfect righteousness of Him Who, though He knew no sin, was made sin for us.

APRIL 23

And they were all filled with the Holy Ghost, and began to speak (Acts 2: 4).

Not for a moment does the inspired record leave us in doubt as to the purpose and outcome of the Spirit's descent at Pentecost. No sooner did He come upon the disciples than they began to speak. Thus we have the principle that Christians are filled with the Spirit in order to witness.

Considered from that point of view, a good deal of praying for the filling of the Spirit is futile. By all means seek a new and more abundant filling, but first of all ask yourself *why* you want the Holy Spirit. Purge your heart of the religious selfishness that seeks Him just so *you* can enjoy new spiritual thrills. Be sure that you desire Him only that you may be a powerful witness to Christ and not to your own spiritual attainments. Above all, remember that it is the Holy Spirit's office to glorify Christ, not men (John 16:14).

APRIL 24

And I beheld, and, lo, in the midst of the Throne and of the four living creatures, and in the midst of the elders, stood a Lamb as it had been slain . . . (Rev. 5: 6).

Symbolical though its expression is, this verse says something of eternal consequence to every soul. It reveals that Christ is the center of Heaven. It shows us that His centrality is eternally linked to His sacrificial work. Had there been no Cross for Christ, He never could have been the Lamb of God. For the unbelieving world the Cross is an offense; the natural man scorns salvation through the Lamb. But God honors the Lamb above all else in the universe; in the midst of His throne He places Christ crucified.

Think, then, about your relationship to the Lamb that was slain. Do you love Him? This one thing is certain: no soul that hates the Christ Who was slain for the sin of the world can ever be in Heaven. Indifference to Him Whom God has made the center of His throne unfits souls for eternity. Do you love the Lamb?

APRIL 25

And the angel of God, which went before the camp of Israel, removed and went behind them; and the pillar of the cloud went from before their face, and stood behind them (Exod. 14:19).

It was time of supreme peril for Israel; the Egyptian host was hard upon them. Hitherto the angel of God and the pillar of cloud had preceded them as their divine Guide. Now danger was imminent. Notice what happened! He Who was their Guidance suddenly turned and went behind them. The angel of God and the pillar of cloud came *between* them and the enemy. Here, then, is a very comforting principle: the Lord Who guides us also defends us. He Who goes before us will not be slow to come behind us when the enemy threatens to overtake us. Know the Lord as your Guide, and you also know Him as your sure Defense.

APRIL 26

Pour out your heart before Him (Ps. 62:8).

This gracious invitation implies certain things in the way of relationship. Not everyone, for instance, would feel free to pour out his heart to his father. Some might be so unfortunate as to have disinterested fathers; others might not feel on sufficiently close terms with their fathers to pour out their hearts to them. The first possibility can never apply to a Christian, for God is a Father Who is always ready to hear His children. But the second possibility applies in many a case. The relationship to the Heavenly Father is broken from the earthly side; the Father is estranged because of the child's wrongdoing. What is the remedy for a broken relationship? Well, when intimacy is lost in a relationship, the way to restore it is simply to resume the intimacy. So those who have felt too far from their Father in Heaven to pour out their hearts to Him must come back to Him in full confession. Then He will restore them to their former tender relationship with Him.

APRIL 27

Abide with us, for it is toward evening, and the day is far spent (Luke 24: 29).

This is the invitation which Cleopas and his companion gave the risen Lord Jesus at the close of the memorable walk to Emmaus. He always responds to such an invitation; whoever says to Christ, "Abide with me," and means what he says, will not receive a refusal. The disciples who met Him on the Emmaus road gave Him this invitation at eventide, when "the day was far spent." And there is a sense in which the day is for all of us "far spent." Though we be young in years, our lives are, as James says, "but a vapour." None of us has any guarantee that this day may not be his last. But, though our days be many or few, the abiding Presence of Christ can hallow them.

"Lord, abide with me." The invitation is one that needs to be renewed daily. Will you not, out of a heart and life set in order for Him, renew that invitation today?

APRIL 28

As He sat at meat with them, He took bread . . . and their eyes were opened, and they knew Him (Luke 24: 30, 31).

When the Lord Jesus answers the invitation of believing hearts, He reveals Himself. And, as we see in these lovely verses, He reveals Himself in the hallowing of common things. The supper which Christ ate with Cleopas and his friend was not the sacrament; it was the plain, everyday supper of an humble home. But, when the Lord touched it with His pierced hand, He transformed it. For in it "their eyes were opened, and they knew Him." Yes, the sanctuary has its place. There is a time for the mountaintop of exalted vision. But most of us deal with the common things; and, if we see Christ only in the moments of ecstasy, we shall have little fellowship with Him. How blessed, therefore, to know that He Who once abode in that humble home long ago will abide with you and me as we go about our daily toil!

APRIL 29

He will rest in His love (Zeph. 3:17).

How much this tells of the attitude of God toward His people! A marginal reading puts it this way: "He will be silent in His love." In either case, it shows that God's controversy with man issues in love. Man has gone astray; he has sinned against God. But God rests His case against man in love, even in His love expressed in Christ. There He is silent; He can do and say no more. That is why there remains for the soul who spurns that love nothing but darkness.

And what about us? Where do we rest our case, our controversy with those who have wronged us? Do we too rest in our love?

APRIL 30

O My people, what have I done unto thee? and wherein have I wearied thee? (Micah 6: 3).

These are holy words; they are the heart cry of a Jehovah Who yearns over His wayward people. Think of it! That God's people should ever fall into the state of being tired of God! Yet is not that exactly what happens to some of us at times? Prayer becomes a heavy burden, public worship is tiresome, even the Word of God bores us. Well, if that is the case, let us remember that the fault is ever with us, never with God. Should Israel be wearied of Jehovah? "Why," He replies, "I brought thee out of the land of Egypt, and redeemed thee out of the house of servants; and I sent before thee Moses, Aaron, and Miriam." And should we be wearied of God when He has done the same for us? He has brought us out of the world to Himself, He has redeemed us from the servitude of sin, He has sent us His ministers to teach us of Himself.

Being weary of God, then, is a symptom of spiritual ill health. It means that there is something in the life which is taking the very heart out of prayer, reading the Word, and public worship. The identity of that thing is between the individual and God. It may be unbelief, or an unforgiving spirit, a hidden sin, or yielding to moods. Whatever the trouble, God will deal with it for you, if you want Him to enough to take the hindrance to Him.

MAY 1

As the hart panteth after the water brooks, so panteth my soul after Thee, O God (Ps. 42:1).

The hart is thirsty because it has been wandering far from the water brook. The soul longs for God when it is distant from Him. So also with the child of God. He may stray away from the streams of living water, but he can never remain away from them for a long time. His soul becomes dry and thirsty, and he hastens back to the fountain of life. We see therefore that there are different ways of undergoing spiritual drouth. True believers wander from the still waters, but their thirst draws them back; the unsaved, never having tasted the water of life, have no thirst for it.

Does this lovely verse portray our own inner longing? Is it true that deep down in our souls we are thirsting after a closer walk with God? Let us remember that what we most truly desire is the measure of what we most truly love.

MAY 2

Behold, the Judge standeth before the door (James 5: 9).

It is very significant to read in this Epistle of James, which is probably the earliest of the New Testament writings, three verses of strong exhortation regarding the return of Christ. Now James does not go into detail as to when or how Christ will return, but he does say unmistakably that He is coming, and he relates that fact to consistent living. And that is the way it should always be with those who are looking for the Lord's return. We Christians may differ as to details of the prophetic picture, but we must be at one in the realization of our personal accountability to Him Who is coming.

"Behold, the Judge standeth at the door." Surely the New Testament contains no more solemn words than those. On the authority of God's Holy Word, on the authority of the great creed, He Who was the meek and lowly Saviour is one day coming again in irresistible power "to judge the quick and the dead." Dear friend, are *you* ready to meet Him, justified by faith and trusting not in yourself but only in His atoning work?

MAY 3

He led them on safely (Ps. 78: 53).

"Safely." That is always the accompaniment of God's leading. He may take you along a perilous path, but when He goes before and points out the way, you are absolutely safe. It is said that the expert Alpine guide can now take even the inexperienced climber safely up the precipitous slopes of the Matterhorn, where several lives were lost on Whymper's first ascent. So the Lord guides you and me safely, always safely, over the steep and dangerous places in our lives. It may be that you are standing today in a hard place and that, as you look ahead, the path appears of impossible difficulty. Never fear. Just trust yourself to your divine Guide, and He will lead you safely.

MAY 4

Pray for them which despitefully use you (Luke 6: 28).

This verse belongs to the forgotten prayer commands of Christ. The Lord Jesus taught at length about prayer, but this is one of the very few instances, aside from the Lord's Prayer, where He expressly enjoined His disciples to pray for a particular thing. There is nothing optional about this word of Christ; it is an imperative command. "Pray," He says, "pray for them which despitefully use you." He leaves no choice and makes no condition. He does not say, "Pray for those who despitefully use you, but wait until they are really repentant." Nor does He say, "Pray only for them who despitefully use you from mistaken motives." It is not for us to whittle down, but simply to obey that command. And let it be remembered that in this instance the Lord Jesus is asking us to do only what He Himself did. For, as He suffered on the Cross, He prayed for those who were despitefully using Him, "Father, forgive them, for they know not what they do."

Everyone of us has at some time or other been despitefully used. And what has thus happened will happen again. But are we really obeying our Lord's command: "Pray for them which despitefully use you"?

MAY 5

The king spake and said unto Daniel, Thy God Whom thou servest continually, He will deliver thee (Dan. 6:16).

"Continually." In that adjective as used of Daniel by King Darius there lies what may well be the greatest compliment ever paid any man of God. There can be little doubt of the close scrutiny under which Daniel lived. Darius was an oriental monarch in a day when plots were common, and Daniel had been officially accused by the subordinate rulers. But Darius' final and considered estimate of Daniel (and it was twice repeated, cf. vs. 10) was summed up in this one statement, "Thy God Whom thou servest continually." What a testimony! For Daniel, life was service of God, and service, life. Let us apply the obvious lesson by asking a question: Is a Christian ever off the duty of his King?

MAY 6

For the love of money is a root of all kinds of evil (I Tim. 6:10, A.S.V.).

This verse, so often misquoted, is an excellent example of the beautiful precision of inspiration. It is not money in itself, but its love that is evil. Nor is the love of money "the root of all evil," as the Authorized Version has it. Evil is like a great, parasitic plant; it puts forth many roots and tendrils of which the love of money is only one. Nevertheless, the verse remains a warning everyone of us needs. Trace evil after evil down to their source, dig them up and look at their roots, and you will find the love of money. It is a sin that has wide ramifications. Your greed may not seem to hurt you, but it may blight your children or your innocent employees. There is hardly a crime, major or minor, that has not at some time been committed for the love of money. For the love of money Balaam sold his prophetic gift; Achan stole the wedge of gold and the Babylonish garment; Gehazi cheated his master, Elisha; Ananias and Sapphira lied to the Holy Ghost; and Judas Iscariot betrayed Christ. There is only one thing strong enough to keep you safe from this most subtle temptation, and that is the constraining love of Christ.

MAY 7

And whatsoever ye do in word or deed, do all in the Name of the Lord Jesus, giving thanks to God and the Father by Him (Col. 3:17).

"Whatsoever" and "all"—two words of broadest inclusiveness, yet Paul uses them to express a thought that definitely excludes many things. For he links the "whatsoever things" and the "all" with the Name of the Lord Jesus. And there are many things that we may not do in the Name of the Lord Jesus. Oh, they may not be downright wrong or sinful. Nevertheless, there is something about them which is quite out of keeping with Him.

Can you find anywhere a safer guide for Christian conduct than this simple rule? Do whatever you wish, provided that you can do it happily in the Name of the Lord Jesus.

MAY 8

And they remained and spent that day with Him (John 1:39, Weymouth).

That one day changed Andrew and his companion. Thenceforth they were different, for they had been with Jesus. The great needs of the human heart do not vary over the centuries. And today as in the first century there is only one companionship that can satisfy the deepest hungers of our hearts. When shall we realize with a force compelling enough to do something about it, that nothing, whether it be preaching, teaching, giving, or even personal witness, can take the place of individual fellowship with the Lord Jesus?

Have you ever spent a day with Him? Do you know what it means to walk with your Lord in heart fellowship? If you have really been with Him, you can never be satisfied for long with any lesser companionship. Let us not forget, Christian friends, that the source of powerful service for our Lord lies in personal knowledge of Him. Fellowship alone with the Lord Jesus is not optional for us Christians; it is as indispensable as the air we breathe.

MAY 9

They sinned still, and believed not for His wondrous works (Ps. 78: 32).

As Asaph continues this marvelous Psalm of God's dealings with His children, there comes this suggestive sentence. Notice that it makes unbelief parallel with sin. "They sinned still" (i.e., they kept on sinning), because they failed to believe.

Now there are different kinds of unbelief. Not every believer on Christ is a believer. That is to say that not every one who believes on the Lord Jesus as his Saviour from sin is really trusting Him fully each day for each day's needs. If he were, there would be no such thing as a worrying Christian. For the Christian who worries is an unbeliever just to the extent in which he worries. Let us not look at unbelief lightly. It is sin to refuse to believe on the Lord Jesus Christ as your Saviour, and it is also sin to continue to doubt His all-sufficiency for your daily need.

MAY 10

Then Job arose . . . and fell down upon the ground, and worshipped (Job 1: 20).

What we do when adversity comes reveals our hold upon God. Job had just received news of the four calamities that wiped out all his wealth and destroyed all his children. His response was one of exemplary spiritual grandeur, for he fell down and worshipped God. Way back in the dim past he knew the New Testament secret of giving thanks in all things and rejoicing in suffering. What about you? Can you take calamity and defeat like a Christian? The world says, "Take defeat and sorrow like a man. Don't give in; keep a stiff upper lip." But God says, "Be like Job. Meet distress not only with fortitude, but above all with worship. Praise Me in your greatest trial, cleave to Me in your darkest hour." O believer, worship will sustain you when the most Spartan heroism will fail.

MAY 11

If any man sin, we have an Advocate with the Father, Jesus Christ the righteous (I John 2:1).

A great Bible teacher has called attention to the exact meaning of the conditional clause with which this sentence begins. It does not read, "If any man confess his sin," or "If any man repent of his sin," or "If any man pray about his sin"; but it says, "If any man sin," *then* the Advocate is at hand to plead his cause before God. How comforting that is. We sin. Weeks or months later we realize our sin and are convicted of it. But long before, even at the very moment when the sin was committed, Jesus Christ the righteous was standing before His Father pleading for us. Oh, how faithful He is in His mediatorial work as our High Priest in Heaven!

MAY 12

The prince of this world cometh, and hath nothing in Me (John 14:30).

If we shall think seriously about these words, they will surely prove a blessing to our souls. By "the prince of this world" our Lord is referring to Satan, who is, according to this and other New Testament teaching, in charge of the present world order. It is, however, the logic implied in this statement that speaks especially to our hearts. If Satan has nothing in Christ, then it is obvious that he has nothing in us, for the Lord Jesus definitely taught in His high-priestly prayer (John 17: 21-23) that we believers are one with the Father in Him. Therefore, since we are united to Christ inseparably, securely, and eternally, Satan, who has no place in Christ, can have no place whatever in us.

Does not this show us the safest way to meet the wiles of the adversary? When he comes at us with his temptations, our surest recourse is simply to fall back upon the blessed truth that we are *in Christ*, in Whom even the prince of this world has nothing.

MAY 13

What shall I render unto the Lord for all His benefits toward me? I will take the cup of salvation (Ps. 116:12, 13).

Here the psalmist is asking the very important question of how a man is to repay God for all His goodness. And the answer to that question is significant. "Take," is the answer. "Take the cup of salvation."

Now there is not a person living, whether sinner or saint, who is not overwhelmingly indebted to God. And the principle of repayment is the same for both sinner and saint. For the unsaved it is, "Take the cup of salvation," which Christ has prepared at infinite cost. For the believer it is still the same—"Take the cup of salvation," for your Lord is a Saviour from the sin of the present as well as from the guilt of the past. Nothing so rejoices the heart of God as simple acceptance of His salvation through Christ; nothing so hurts and dishonors Him as for a sinful man to spurn that salvation. Have you taken, are you taking today that cup of His salvation?

MAY 14

Therefore the Jews sought the more to kill Him, because He not only had broken the Sabbath, but said also that God was His Father, making Himself equal with God (John 5:18).

Twisted spiritual values are never unimportant. Sooner or later they manifest themselves in life. And sometimes they lead to dreadful consequences, as in this case. The Jews, the very people to whom Christ came as King, sought avidly to slay Him. Why? What was the genesis of their hatred that led to the greatest crime of the ages? Simply warped spiritual judgment. They considered their hidebound Sabbath restrictions of more value than deeds of mercy; legalism had so blinded them that they failed to recognize the only begotten Son of God.

But are we better than they? In no wise, when it comes to our unaided human nature. Only the Spirit of Christ, dwelling in our hearts by faith, can give us the clarity of spiritual sight that will enable us to place first things first.

MAY 15

This man is the great power of God (Acts 8:10).

These were dangerous words that the people of Samaria applied to Simon Magus. So striking were his magical arts and so fascinated did the people become that they went to the terrible extreme of identifying the sorcerer with the actual power of God. There was, of course, only One Who could properly claim to be in Himself the power of God. But have you ever noticed that even our Lord Himself was always careful to give the glory to His Father?

Think of the grace of God in making us Christians the vehicles for the power of His Holy Spirit! How we should rejoice that He is working in us, and at the same time how scrupulously careful we should be to repudiate even the slightest suggestion that would attribute to us any of the power that comes from God alone!

MAY 16

A faithful man shall abound with blessings: but he that maketh haste to be rich shall not be innocent (Prov. 28: 20).

Like so many verses in Proverbs this statement contains a wealth of practical wisdom. It meets the test of reality, for its assertions have over and over again been proved true in human life. Let us notice that riches are not promised the faithful man. The promise is of abundance of blessings, and these may not be of a material nature. The great fact is that God does reward faithfulness to Himself and to His Word with blessing. And how shrewdly wise is the last clause! Life proves that when a man hastens to be rich he is all too liable to lose his innocence. For there is something about the headlong pursuit of wealth that corrodes integrity.

The spiritual lesson is that there is but one objective a man or woman may safely pursue with utmost zeal and self-abandonment. That objective is the will of God. Other all-absorbing goals, whether riches or fame, learning or art, may in some way lead to moral deterioration. But those who make haste to serve the Lord will find themselves constantly drawing closer to Him Whom they are serving.

MAY 17

Now the God of hope fill you with all joy and peace in believing (Rom. 15:13).

We all want more joy and peace in our hearts. And in these words Paul tells us very briefly how we may obtain them. Their source, of course, is "the God of hope" Who fills us with all joy and peace. But the channel through which He pours out these incomparable spiritual boons is "believing." "In (or 'by') believing"—that is the sure way to receive more joy and peace in your life today. Believe in the promise of the God of peace (Heb. 13:20), trust fully in Him, and into your heart will flow His joy and His peace. Believe in the faithfulness of your God and you *will* have peace and joy — not outward calm or happiness which are very different things — but that inner peace and joy which only His loved ones know.

MAY 18

Everyone is looking for You (Mark 1: 37, Weymouth).

The Lord Jesus had left the house early in the morning to go alone to pray. Simon and the others searched for Him, and when they found Him, this is what they said, "Everyone is looking for You."

Those words are true of thousands and millions all about us. Far from Christ, vainly seeking to live their own lives in their own strength, they are yet looking for Him. Because they have Him not, they are restless, unhappy, starved and hopeless. If they could only learn that the Object of their perverse and futile striving is so willing to be found!

It is the glory of the Gospel witness that it points bewildered and lost men and women to the One for Whom they are looking. We ask the question of the unbeliever, "Have you found Christ?" But it is not Christ, but the unbeliever who is lost. Proclaiming the exceeding sinfulness of sin and bringing the lost to a conviction of their ruin in transgression, this opens their hearts to Him for Whom they have unconsciously been looking and Who will come in and find them.

MAY 19

Hear, all ye people; hearken, O earth (Micah 1:2).

Thus does the prophet Micah begin the messages God gave through him. And thus does the word of God come to us, thousands of years after Micah. "Hear, hearken," God and His prophets are crying. But man stops his ears against the arresting call of God. Voices are all about us, seeking our attention and allegiance. On the one hand, the world calls with alluring insistence; on the other hand, self clamors, day in and day out. And all the time God is saying, "Hear Me, hearken unto Me." You say that you *have* heard Him. Very well, but look back over the past week. Ask yourself this question: In all my decisions, large and small, in all my preferences and choices, have I been heeding God's voice or the voice of another?

MAY 20

I was no prophet, neither was I a prophet's son: but I was an herdman, and a gatherer of sycomore fruit: and the Lord took me as I followed the flock, and the Lord said unto me, Go, prophesy . . . (Amos 7:14, 15).

Thus answered Amos before Amaziah. Out of a lowly herdman God made a prophet whose denunciations of sin and corruption have echoed down the ages. Who you are by birth or social position means much to the world; it means little to a sovereign God. From cover to cover the Bible drives home the truth that God delights to use unpromising material and shape it into powerful instruments for His service. The greatest failures in the Bible, such as Samson, Saul, and Solomon, had everything in their favor at the beginning. It is not native talent or birth with a silver spoon in the mouth that qualifies one for God's service. It is submission to His will. Average or even mediocre ability plus full consecration will accomplish far more for Christ than sheer genius not completely yielded to His will. For it is not human genius that brings spiritual harvest, but God's own power; and that power demands a submissive human instrument through whom to work.

MAY 21

How can we know the way?... I am the Way (John 14:5, 6).

Have you never asked the question of Thomas? Have you never cried out in your bewilderment, "How can I know the way?" Surely you have, for one of the most constant needs of the Christian life is the need of guidance. Well, the answer is the same today as when the Lord Jesus gave it to Thomas. "I am the Way." Yes, He is the Way. Seek Christ, first and always, and you will find the Way. Find Him and you find guidance in every perplexity. Oh, when shall we learn more perfectly the divinely simple secret of the Christian life—the secret that the Lord Jesus is all and in all! *He* is our guidance.

MAY 22

But as soon as this thy son was come . . . thou hast killed for him the fatted calf. And he said unto him, Son . . . this thy brother was dead, and is alive again (Luke 15:30-32).

Let us look at some of the undertones of this marvelous parable. The elder brother speaks out of a heart full of selfish malice. Referring to the prodigal, he contemptuously calls him, "this thy son." In his bitter self-righteousness, he abjures the brotherly bond. How graciously the father answers his surly firstborn. No venom of the elder brother prevents the loving father from addressing him as "Son." And how tenderly the father pleads for the prodigal as "thy brother," thus commending him to the hardened heart of the elder son.

Forget that your fellow man is your brother, and "the milk of human kindness" will dry up within you. Your heavenly Father will not abjure His intimate relationship with you, O Christian. Why then should you draw aside your cloak from your sinning brother or sister? We need to remember, we fortunate ones enjoying the privilege of heirship through Christ, that there is no record of the elder brother's participation in the joyous welcome of the prodigal. His jealous narrowness evidently shut him out as effectively as the other's wandering had kept him away from his father's house.

MAY 23

Here am I, my son (Gen. 22:7).

It is only the word of a human father, but how it speaks of the Heavenly Father! The occasion was a tragic one. Abraham was about to offer up his son, Isaac, as a sacrifice. And Isaac, all unconscious that he was the sacrifice, was calling upon his father to ask where the lamb was. "My father," was his cry. Then Abraham replied, "Here am I, my son." He was ready to help his son, even though he saw no way of escape from the sacrifice.

But where Abraham was helpless, the Heavenly Father is powerful. Had not God intervened, Isaac might indeed have been slain. But God provided the ram for the offering. And He will *always* respond to the cry of Isaac. Let us call upon God. He will answer us. To our "my Father," He ever replies, "Here am I, My child."

MAY 24

Put on the whole armour of God, that ye may be able to stand against the wiles of the devil (Eph. 6:11).

One reason why there are so many defeated Christians is that they are daring to enter upon spiritual warfare incompletely protected. God has, Paul tells us in this magnificent passage, provided us believers with His *whole* armor. And that armor is absolutely sufficient for our entire protection. We cannot leave off a single piece of it and remain safe. Foolhardy indeed is the Christian who ventures upon even one day without the girdle of truth, the breastplate of righteousness, the shoes of the gospel of peace, the shield of faith, the helmet of salvation, and the sword of the Spirit, which is the Word of God.

The trouble is that some of us are preoccupied with but one piece of God's armor to the extent that others are neglected. Yes, we may be experts in the use of the sword of the Spirit and still be defeated because we have forgotten the shield of faith. Think it over, Christian friend. Are you wearing the *whole* armor of God?

MAY 25

Therefore put to death your earthward inclinations. . . .
But now you must rid yourselves of every kind of sin (Col.
3: 5-8, Weymouth).

The apostle here becomes very specific as to our part in
this matter of dying to sin. In principle the old, sinful nature
was crucified with Christ on Calvary. But we have to realize
practically what happened in principle nineteen hundred years
ago. Christ has taken sin's penalty away. And we, so long as
we are in this earthly life, must be willing to crucify our earthward inclinations and thus to rid ourselves of every kind of sin.

It is a wholesome spiritual exercise to take these verses
and their context, wherein are mentioned some very definite
things, and to say to God in prayer that you are willing to
have any of those things that are in your life nailed to the
cross, however great the cost may be to you. Yes, you will
have to do this more than once, for sin dies slowly. But
Christ will help you put these things to death.

MAY 26

Nevertheless we, according to His promise, look for new
heavens and a new earth, wherein dwelleth righteousness.
Wherefore, beloved, seeing that ye look for such things, be
diligent (II Peter 3:13, 14).

In Peter's dealing with the sure fact of the return of Christ,
there is a wonderful strain of practicality. So often the
charge is made against advent truth that it is other-worldly
and impractical; that it is dangerous to lift our eyes in ex-
pectation of our Lord's coming, for it diverts our attention
from the every day duties of life.

How completely Peter answers this objection! He says in
effect that we believers are looking for a new order of things,
characterized by righteousness. Therefore, seeing that we
have a new heaven and earth in which righteousness will be
preëminent, we must be "diligent" to live righteously at this
present time. In this connection, F. W. Grant makes an apt
comment. "How unsuitable," he exclaims, "for the looking
for this condition of perfect righteousness would be the least
laxity with regard to it now!"

MAY 27

The heavens declare the glory of God; and the firmament showeth His handiwork (Ps. 19:1).

"The heavens declare." But do you ever stop to listen to them? God speaks in His written Word, and commands our attention. But He has another Book, the Book of Nature, wherein is declared His glory. "The invisible things of Him from the creation of the world are clearly seen, being understood by the things that are made" (Rom. 1:20). You and I are not doing full honor to God if we fail to listen to what His wonderful universe says of His greatness. It is a blessed thing to study the handiwork of God.

MAY 28

He brought me up also out of an horrible pit, out of the miry clay, and set my feet upon a rock, and established my goings (Ps. 40: 2).

When a man is in the horrible pit of sin and his feet are mired in the clay of iniquity, he cannot help himself. Good advice can never lift him out, high ideals are powerless to extricate his feet. He needs someone outside himself and outside the pit wherein he is fallen to help him. Thus we see that only Christ can do what this verse so vividly portrays. For Christ only is outside the pit of sin in that He alone of all the sons of men was sinless. A Confucius or a Buddha may offer moral advice to the fallen sinner. None but Christ has ever gone down into the pit of sin, lifted out the sinner, and set his feet upon the solid rock.

This is His unique work of redemption. Quite rightly we believers think of it as finished, for Christ has once and for all set our feet upon Himself, the solid rock. Yet the last words of the verse say something about the present. As Young translates them, they literally read, "He is establishing my steps." The thought is that of His blessed supervision of our steps here and now. He Who has set our feet upon the rock will see that we continue to walk upon the rock. He Himself is establishing our steps and He sees to it that we shall not slip back into the miry clay and fall again into the horrible pit.

MAY 29

Which of you convinceth Me of sin? (John 8: 46).

Spoken nineteen hundred years ago, that question has never been answered. No man ever lived who was subjected to more hostile scrutiny than Christ. The eagle eyes of evil men, sharpened by the malice of the devil, watched Him day and night. Throughout the intervening years His enemies have sifted every record to discover one doubtful word or unsanctified act. Yet none has ever arisen or ever will arise to demonstrate a single sin in Christ. His unanswerable challenge, "Which of you convinceth Me of sin?" stands as an overwhelming proof of the perfection of His Person.

"What a Friend we have in Jesus!" When men disappoint us, as even the best of them will; when those we trusted fail us; when the greatest prove small, and the strongest weak; what a comfort it is to turn to Christ and know that *in Him* we have a *perfect* Lord!

MAY 30

These things understood not His disciples at the first: but when Jesus was glorified, then remembered they that these things were written of Him, and that they had done these things unto Him (John 12:16).

Would we begin really to understand our Lord? Then we must use this key: "*When* Jesus was glorified, *then* remembered they . . ." There, in His glorification, is the key to understanding our Lord.

Why is it that, for so very many, Christ is only a lovely religious figure, hidden behind pious phrases, remote from our daily round as the dimly beautiful cathedral window? Let us ask ourselves another question and we shall have the answer. Is Christ being glorified in our lives? When we come to the place of personally glorifying Him, then we shall begin to understand what Christ can mean to us. "The Holy Spirit was not yet given, because that Jesus was not yet glorified" (John 7:39). There lies the source of the powerlessness of many a professing Christian today. Unless Jesus is glorified by being given the preëminence in a believer's heart, there simply cannot be any true understanding of what He can mean to the individual life.

MAY 31

*Live thus, realizing the situation, that it is now high time
to rouse yourselves from sleep; for our salvation is now nearer
than when we first became believers* (Rom. 13:11, Weymouth).

There is probably no single thing that hinders the work
of God in this generation more than the spiritual sluggishness
of believers. The preacher knows it, as he sees such placid
Christians sitting in the pews. Oh, they receive his message
very politely and they listen with quiet respect, but how dull
their perceptions and slow their spirits. While all about
them rings the challenge of the unsaved, they are content to
remain half awake, formally acknowledging the power of
the Gospel, but just not taking the trouble really to wake
up and do something about it.

What is the remedy? Well, we may talk about the past
or speculate about the future, but we cannot escape the
present. We Christians must cultivate a sense of contempo-
raneity; we have an obligation to be alive to the very hour
in which we live. The New Testament gives little comfort
to those who think religion means withdrawing from the life
about them. Perilous though our times may be, they are
a challenge to active service as good soldiers of Jesus Christ.
So Paul uses the phrase, "Knowing the time," or, as Weymouth translates it, "realizing the situation." And then he
exhorts us believers to wake up because now, this very day,
our salvation is nearer than when we first believed, nearer
because we are daily drawing closer to the culmination of
our salvation when we shall meet our Saviour face to face.
All eternity will be ours to spend with our Lord and rest
in the joy of His presence. But there are given to us only
these few short hours to serve Him through proclaiming His
Gospel to the lost. Let us wake up and live for Christ!

> *Awake, my soul, stretch every nerve,*
> *And press with vigor on;*
> *A heavenly race demands thy zeal,*
> *And an immortal crown.*

JUNE 1

And he said unto them, Set your hearts unto all the words which I testify among you this day . . . all the words of this law. For it is not a vain thing for you; because it is your life (Deut. 32: 46, 47).

At the conclusion of the great discourses of Deuteronomy wherein are summarized God's holy law and His dealings with His people, Moses gives this exhortation. Let us mark well the significance of these words: "It is your life." The reference is to the Word of God as given through Moses. That Word is not a vain thing for God's people. It is their very life.

What was true of Israel and the Pentateuch certainly applies to Christians and the Bible. If the inspired words of Moses were the life of the chosen people, the whole Word of God is vital to us. Indeed it is very doubtful whether one can consider the Bible a vain thing and at the same time be a Christian. "Set your hearts unto all the words" applies to us in our every day use of the Bible.

JUNE 2

Grieve not the Holy Spirit of God (Eph. 4:30).

If we are to understand this solemn warning, we must remember Who the Holy Spirit is and where He dwells. A low view of the Holy Spirit regards Him as just an inspirational adjunct occasionally stirring up religious emotion. But a high and scriptural view recognizes His Deity. For He is verily, as Paul says, the Holy Spirit *of God*, and it is just as wrong to deny His Deity as it is to deny the Deity of Christ. And it is the plain teaching of the New Testament that none other than this Divine and Holy Spirit dwells within the heart of every Christian believer.

Think on those things, and order your life today accordingly. When the hasty word comes to your tongue, remember that the Holy Spirit will hear it and be grieved by it. When you incline to some selfish indulgence, recollect that the Divine Guest Whose temple you are, will witness what you do. The forgotten fundamental of the faith is the doctrine of the Holy Spirit. Let you and me remember Him that we may not grieve but rejoice Him in all things.

JUNE 3

Thy faith hath saved thee; go in peace (Luke 7: 50).

Considered in the light of the beautiful narrative they conclude, these words are startling. For in Luke's account of the woman who brought to Christ the alabaster box of ointment and washed his feet with tears, wiping them with her hair, there is no mention of the fact that she said a single word. True, conversation is recorded, but it is between Christ and His host, Simon the Pharisee. Yet here is the Lord's declaration that the woman's faith had saved her.

Surely this is an impressive answer to the thought that talking is enough. There are times when faith is best witnessed by deed rather than by word. The woman did something. What she did was so believing, so permeated with faith, that it has come down the ages as a memorial to her. Let her faith, mutely but powerfully expressed, challenge us to a practical as well as verbal witness to our Lord.

JUNE 4

But ye have not so learned Christ (Eph. 4: 20).

"Ye have not learned Christ," writes Paul, and with these striking words points back to the sinful manner of life which characterizes the unsaved and which he has just described. Just because the old nature is present with us, drawing us back to the old, sinful life; just because temptation constantly assails; just because the devil is always soliciting us to evil; we Christians ought to lay these words of Paul very close to our hearts. Oh, the reproach they bring after we have sinned! *"Ye have not so learned Christ* as to fall back into that sin, forsaken by you when you were saved." *"Ye have not so learned Christ* as to be so self-seeking, even in doing His work." *"Ye have not so learned Christ* as to succumb to fear and worry, when you know assuredly that your God is able perfectly to take care of His children." Thus the Word is speaking to your heart and mine and wooing us away from the old life of worldly, sinful indulgence.

JUNE 5

But we have the mind of Christ (I Cor. 2:16).

Suppose that you were assured of having the mind of Aristotle or Plato, Newton or Bacon with which to solve your problems. Suppose that for your literary needs the mind of Shakespeare or Milton were available to you. Would you not be overjoyed at your good fortune? But these are but feeble comparisons of what you actually have, O Christian! For you have the mind of Christ! Think of it; that matchless mind of the Lord Jesus is available for your help and guidance. How sad, then, that you make so little use of it. Elsewhere, the apostle Paul says, "Let this mind be in you, which was also in Christ Jesus" (Phil. 2:5). But are you doing it? Are you letting the mind of Christ actually be *in* you? There is only one way to do that. It is not by striving, but by believing; not by working, but by submitting; not by trying, but by yielding. Give Christ complete control of your life, and you will have His mind in you.

JUNE 6

[They] have no root in themselves, and so endure but for a time: afterward, when affliction or persecution ariseth for the Word's sake, immediately they are offended (Mark 4:17).

How quickly are you offended? How easily do you give up in your spiritual life? These questions come to mind through a meditation upon this passage from the familiar parable of the sower. Our Lord is describing certain religious persons who, when things go well, endure. However, just as soon as affliction and persecution arise for the Word's sake, these persons are *immediately* offended. Notice that the affliction referred to is that which comes because of a specific thing; it is persecution *for the Word's sake*. This clearly means that there must have been some prior testimony on the part of those whom the Lord is describing. They lacked, however, plain endurance; their roots were just too shallow.

How deep do your spiritual roots go? If you would not be immediately and easily offended by persecution and affliction, your life must have a hidden root system striking way down into God's truth and deriving nourishment from Him.

JUNE 7

He knew all men . . . He knew what was in [the heart of]
man (John 2: 24, 25).

True friendship means intimacy. One of the tests of a
friend is when he knows the worst about you. If, knowing
the worst, he still loves you, he is indeed your friend. Yet
there are things in all of us that we would not dare have
any human friend know. Is it not wonderful, however, that
there is one Friend Who does know these things, and knowing
them, still loves us with an undying love? The Lord Jesus
knows all men. This very day, just as in John's day, He knows
what is in man. And the marvel of it is that, knowing the
heart of man and its inherent evil (Mark 7: 21-23), He loved
us enough to die for us. "Greater love hath no man than this,
that a man lay down his life for his friend." Read that in
the light of the Lord Jesus' knowledge of our hearts and you
will wonder at it anew. "What a Friend we have in Jesus!"

JUNE 8

Yea, and all that will live godly in Christ Jesus shall
suffer persecution (II Tim. 3:12).

This verse states the principle that all who are determined
to live for Christ must pay a price. Paul was not speaking
by way of simple futurity; he was not just saying that all
who in the natural course of time will be living godly lives
will be persecuted. On the contrary, he used the very definite
word, *thelo*, meaning "to resolve, determine, or purpose."

The underlying principle is this: Everyone who determines
in his heart to "live godly in Christ Jesus" must pay the
price. And that price is persecution. Thus must it be so
long as the adversary remain. Satan is not interested in per-
secuting half-way Christians who have not resolutely set
themselves to live godly; he knows they will never amount
to anything. But he does persecute the believer who by a
definite act of will has determined to follow his Lord.

Yes, Christian friend, it is not surprising that you are
suffering. It would rather be surprising if you were not
meeting some form of testing. But just remember that like
Paul you too will sometimes say of your trials and persecutions: "But out of them *all* the Lord delivered me" (vs. 11).

JUNE 9

*The Lord will strengthen him upon the bed of languishing:
Thou wilt make all his bed in his sickness* (Ps. 41:3).

If there is ever a time when God is near, it is when we
are ill. Some of our greatest spiritual blessings come when
we are laid aside from the daily round. For the believer
sickness is not an unmixed calamity. In the moments when
weakness and pain prevent even such mild occupations as
reading, God is near and speaking to His child. While it
may not always be His will to strengthen the body, He ever
works to strengthen the soul of the afflicted believer. It is
impossible for a child of God to suffer illness with a submissive will and not be spiritually blessed. Many a choice
Christian has learned his deepest spiritual lessons in bodily
weakness. Let us remember that when God makes our bed
in our sickness, as the psalmist beautifully phrases it, He may
be sending us to His school of advanced instruction in the
life of the soul.

JUNE 10

*But they measuring themselves by themselves, and compar-
ing themselves among themselves, are not wise* (II Cor. 10:12).

It matters a very great deal by what standard a Christian
judges himself. Paul says that certain members of the Church
at Corinth were unwise in their method of self-appraisal.
Are you also unwise in this respect? Are you measuring yourself by yourself, are you comparing yourself with other Christians, either to your self-praise or self-condemnation? Do not
do it. It is dangerous to look to men, and the most dangerous of all men to whom you may look is yourself. There is
another measure and a better standard. Look to the Son of
man. When you need an appraisal, turn your eyes to "Jesus,
the Author and Finisher of your faith." Remember that He
said, "Be ye perfect," and that, though only He fully exem-
plifies God's standard, He has made provision through your
faith in His blood for you ultimately to reach in Him the
heavenly measure of His righteousness.

JUNE 11

Seek ye out of the book of the Lord (Isa. 34:16).

That is something everyone of us needs to do every day. Our daily bread is important, but more important is the book of the Lord. God has joined certain things forever, and among them are guidance and the Word of God. Similarly He has united the Word and spiritual growth. "What therefore God hath joined together let not man put asunder" (Matt. 19:6) was spoken in quite another connection, yet it applies in this case.

Are you trying to separate Christian growth and guidance from God's Word? Then you are putting asunder things that God has joined. The only way to live the Christian life is daily to obey Isaiah's inspired counsel, "Seek ye out of the book of the Lord."

JUNE 12

Jesus Christ (He is Lord of all) (Acts 10:36).

This is a significant parenthesis that Peter includes in his sermon in the house of Cornelius. Consider it as a statement of unassailable fact, for such it is. He (Jesus Christ) is Lord of all. That is His God-given, actual place in the universe. "But," someone objects, "how about the unbelievers? How about the millions who are in ignorance of Him? How about the nations today who are definitely opposed to Him?" Yes, there are hosts of unbelievers and millions who have never heard Christ's name. And there are nations who are opposed to Him. But still He *is* Lord of all. A President is head of this country; even though there are those who oppose him, he is still their President. In some remote corner of an Empire there may be some subjects of a king who have not yet heard of their ruler's accession. But he is nevertheless their sovereign. So Christ *is* Lord of all, though in many cases He is not yet acknowledged as such.

The vital question is whether He is your Lord. You are first of all responsible for your personal submission to Him. It is folly to think of bringing others under His sovereignty, if He does not have full sway over you.

JUNE 13

And he brought him to Jesus (John 1:42).

Andrew is the subject of this sentence, and it is Peter whom he brought to Jesus. We know comparatively little of Andrew, but, on the basis of what we do know about him, it is safe to say that he never did anything greater than when he brought his own brother, Peter, to Christ.

What have you done with your brother or sister, father or mother? What have you done with your friends? Have you brought them to Jesus? "Oh," you say, "my dear ones are already saved." Well, you may praise God for that. Yet do not forget that you may still bring them to Jesus in prayer for their blessing day by day. And surely there are some close to you who are still unsaved. You may bring them to Jesus by a direct word of witness, as did Andrew with Peter (vs. 41). And you may also and very urgently bring them to Him in prayer. Whatever else you may be doing, are you, Christian friend, bringing individuals to Jesus?

JUNE 14

That ye may know . . . what is the exceeding greatness of His power to us-ward who believe (Eph. 1:18, 19).

The inspiration of the Scriptures is a very practical truth. It bids us look deep into God's Word, and encourages us to find food for our souls in even the smaller details of divine revelation. For, once a Christian grants the inspiration of the Bible, he will not find it hard to take the logical step that, although there may be obscurities and difficulties in the Word, God does not inspire trivialities. So let us look today at a preposition. Translated by the archaic "to us-ward," it is in Greek the little word *eis*. Obviously it is a word of direction. And what a message the Holy Spirit packed into it, as Paul penned it in this place in Ephesians! "The exceeding greatness of His power *to us-ward* who believe." Think of it! The omnipotence of the Almighty is directed straight toward us, provided that (and the proviso is of cardinal importance) we believe. How sad that we should ever allow our wretched unbelief to deflect this power from its appointed destination in our needy lives!

JUNE 15

If thou hast thought evil, lay thine hand upon thy mouth (Prov. 30: 32).

The author of this statement lived nearly three thousand years ago, but the most advanced psychology cannot improve upon his advice. How different our personal relationships would be, were we consistently to heed it. Thoughts of evil are bound to come into our minds, but if we will just seal our lips against their utterance, we shall be delivered from a vast amount of trouble not only for ourselves but for others. No one is responsible for thoughts contrary to truth and righteousness; the devil is adept in the insertion of his temptations into the mind. But everyone of us is responsible for dwelling upon thoughts of evil. And the moment we open our mouths to give life to these thoughts by putting them into words, we are doubly responsible. Many an evil thought is as truly thwarted by the closed mouth as the electric current is stopped by the glass insulator.

JUNE 16

We know what love is because He laid down His life for us; and we ought to lay down our lives for our brethren. But if anyone has this world's goods and sees that his brother is in need, and yet closes his heart against him—how can the love of God continue in him? (I John 3:16, 17, Weymouth).

John's logic is inescapable. Its major premise is based upon the fact that Christ has taught us what sacrificial love is. Indeed, we are not Christians unless we have personally learned that lesson. There is, John is saying, only one fit response to the sacrificial love of Christ for us. That is that we should lay down our lives for the brethren. In particular, he asks how anyone whom God has blessed with worldly goods can close his heart to his brother's need and still claim to be indwelt by the love of God.

In view of these pointed words the comparatively little that Christians give to the alleviation of physical and spiritual suffering constitutes one of the major scandals of the church. No amount of pious talk and theological discussion will ever do away with that scandal. Let us be sure that not one of us is ever under the reproach of closing his heart to the needy. In this case actions speak louder than words.

JUNE 17

*The Gospel which was preached of me is not after man.
For I neither received it of man, neither was I taught it,
but by the revelation of Jesus Christ* (.Gal. 1:11, 12).

After all, what was true of Paul holds for everybody else.
There is but one way to apprehend the Gospel, and that is
"by the revelation (literally, 'unveiling') of Jesus Christ."
To be sure, the Gospel was revealed to Paul in a special way,
and we cannot expect the same manner of revelation. Yet no
one apprehends the Gospel without an unveiling of Christ,
whether through a sermon, or a testimony, through the Word,
or through the direct operation of the Spirit in the heart.
Back of it all there *must* be a personal revelation of Christ
in His work as sin-bearer for anyone to get the Gospel in
His heart.

Has Christ been thus revealed to you? If so, is the testimony of your life a revelation of Him?

JUNE 18

*That He might be just and the justifier of him which be-
lieveth in Jesus* (Rom. 3: 26).

God, the Almighty Sovereign, faced the greatest problem
in the universe. It was this: How can a righteous, holy God
justify the guilty sinner? Or, as Paul puts it, how can He remain just and yet be the justifier of the sinner? That problem
was solved on the Cross. It was on the accursed tree that
the solution was worked out with nails and a spear thrust.
In a way that the unbelieving world still calls foolishness,
God solved that staggering moral equation. In Christ, smitten
for the sins of many, He remained just and became the
justifier of the believing sinner.

Granted that, and if you are a Christian you *must* grant
it, some very important conclusions follow. If it was not too
hard a problem for God to justify you, there is no difficulty
in your life with which He is not able to deal. Compared
with the saving of your soul, the breaking of a habit, victory
over sin, or the giving of wisdom to the perplexed—any
one of these is a small thing. Oh, that we might rest firm
on the foundation that in Him is found the solution of our
every problem, the meeting of our every need!

JUNE 19

And because iniquity shall abound, the love of many shall wax cold (Matt. 24:12).

These words from our Lord's Olivet Discourse set forth the severe logic of cause and effect. Spiritual coldness always bears a direct relationship to iniquity. Iniquity has a protean quality; it ranges from grossly indulged sin to subtle unbelief. But whatever be its form, when it is tolerated in a Christian's life it leads to coldness in spiritual things. The believer who is leaving his first love for Christ is one who is becoming too familiar with some form of iniquity. When we find our love for our Lord waxing cold, let us be diligent in rooting out the cause of that blighting chill.

JUNE 20

Finally, my brethren, be strong in the Lord, and in the power of His might (Eph. 6:10).

Life in this modern world is making exorbitant demands upon human strength with the result that the casualties in shattered nerves, weakened bodies, and sick souls are sadly numerous. And so our hope for living on the highest level lies in learning the secret of strength. Our verse for today is, then, of immense practical value, for it speaks very plainly of overcoming strength.

"My brethren," cries Paul, "be strong *in the Lord, and in the power of His might.*" Now Paul was naturally a strong man. But he learned that mere vigor of mind and body can never win out in the Christian warfare. Wherefore we find him saying elsewhere, "When I am weak, then am I strong" (II Cor. 12:10). Through affliction God had taught him the meaning of these words: "My strength is made perfect in weakness." That lesson meant for Paul living with "a thorn in the flesh." But what power it released in his life and ministry!

You are discouraged or tired or fearful, Christian friend? Where, then, are you going for strength? Oh, learn with Paul that you can be strong *in the Lord, and in the power of His might.* Your time of greatest weakness may become through Him your time of maximum strength.

JUNE 21

Do as Thou hast said (II Sam. 7:25).

David uttered these words in his prayer after God made His covenant with him. "Do as Thou hast said." If only we might learn to make that petition the groundtone of our prayer-life! Have you ever thought how in actual practice we reverse it? Piously we say, "Yea, Lord, Thy will be done," but all the time the burden of our prayers is "O Lord, do as I have said." How foolish! It matters little what we have said; God has spoken. He has spoken fully in His Word. And the highest we can ask for others and for ourselves is to have Him do exactly as He has said. Oh, to have our prayer-life rooted and grounded in His "exceeding great and precious promises"!

JUNE 22

At that time Berodach-baladan, the son of Baladan, king of Babylon, sent letters and a present unto Hezekiah: for he had heard that Hezekiah had been sick (II Kings 20:12).

Here begins the record of how a great saint may fall! Faced with violence Hezekiah was brave; in the presence of death he was humbly trustful. But before the blandishments of flattery he fell. For he listened to the smooth words of Berodach-baladan and exhibited all the treasures of his realm, thus stirring cupidity in the Babylonian breast and paving the way for the coming invasion and captivity. "And Hezekiah hearkened unto them, and showed them all the house of his precious things . . . there was nothing in his house, nor in all his dominion that Hezekiah showed them not" (vs. 13). Why did Hezekiah fall prey to this snare of the devil? Because of his pride! Vain in his possessions, he showed them off before profane eyes. So we see that there are some things God's people must not share with the world. There are quiet places in the life of the soul, and hallowed thoughts which, when shared with those who are without, tend to vanity and become an occasion for sin. In every Christian life there is a place for holy reticence.

JUNE 23

He is able to succour them that are tempted (Heb. 2:18).

This comforting verse is universal: "Them that are tempted" includes all humanity. Everybody, even our divine Lord, has had to meet temptation. And that is just the reason why He is so fully able to succour the tempted. Not only after the forty day fast in the wilderness, but all through His life upon earth Satan attacked Him. Yet never once, in thought, word, or deed, did He yield. Thus the Lord Jesus knows our every weakness. He is the true Friend of sinners, because "He Himself hath suffered being tempted." He understands our trials, because He Himself faced the tempter. He knows the path of victory, because He defeated the tempter in everything.

Dear friend, no matter what your temptation may be, no matter how great your trial is, be assured that the Lord Jesus is able to succour you. His understanding help is available for you this very day. But to receive it you must cease to depend upon yourself and look instead to Christ alone.

JUNE 24

Let your forbearance be known to all men; the Lord is near (Phil. 4:5, Young's Literal Translation).

How much this verse has to say to those of us who are inclined to be intolerant and impatient! Our forbearance or "gentleness," as the marginal reading has it, is to be manifest to all, because the Lord is near. And His nearness means that He is at hand to help in every situation. In nothing are we believers without Him Who is ever near us. And when in the course of our human relationships something arises to tempt us to impatience or indignation or intolerance, our balance wheel lies in the knowledge that He Who is able to deal perfectly with everything and everybody is at hand.

All too rare among us believers is the quietness of spirit which avoids emotional and temperamental extremes. We shall indeed make greater progress in Christian living if we will earnestly cultivate the forbearance and gentleness derived from reliance upon our Lord Who, being always near, is thus ever available for every circumstance.

JUNE 25

Oh that my words were now written! oh that they were printed in a book! That they were graven with an iron pen and lead in the rock forever (Job 19: 23, 24).

And this wish of Job has also come true! His words are indeed printed in a book. They are graven forever not just in the rock, but upon the enduring substance of eternal souls. Job's words are indestructible, because they are words of supreme faith. The man who, back in the dim ages of the past, exclaimed, "I know that my Redeemer liveth, and that He shall stand at the latter day upon the earth" (vs. 25), spoke inspired words that will endure forever. Out of his bitter affliction came imperishable words of trust in God. And as for us, shall we not learn that the most enduring deeds we can do, the most abiding words we can speak are the deeds and words based upon faith in God and His faithfulness?

JUNE 26

In the day when I cried Thou answeredst me, and strengthenedst me with strength in my soul (Ps. 138:3).

This is a true testimony of the way in which God works in man's extremity. We do not know whether David was referring to some particular deliverance in his eventful life or whether he was thinking of a long series of deliverances. But we do know that he gives a real witness to God's method of dealing with our cries for help. First, there is the fact that God answers the prayer for help. Just how He answers is secondary; whether He immediately intervenes in a tangible way or whether He simply gives the assurance that He has heard the prayer, the fact is that He answers the heart-cry of His people. And then He does more; He strengthens His people where they most need to be strengthened—*in their souls*. Many are the times when God must answer negatively some petition close to our hearts. Yet, though the thorn has to remain in our flesh, our God imparts strength to our very souls, and says to us, as He said to Paul, "My grace is sufficient for thee: for My strength is made perfect in weakness" (II Cor. 12:9).

JUNE 27

For how great is His goodness, and how great is His beauty (Zech. 9:17).

Notice the word with which this exclamation of worship begins. "For" is a signpost, always pointing in one direction —backwards. And whenever we exclaim, as we often should, at the goodness and beauty of our God, we are turning our eyes backwards. His goodness is known to us through the gracious ways in which He has already dealt with us; His beauty is seen through His revelation of Himself. Amid the infinite diversities of human life, there is one thing we all have in common. It is our past. And different though the past be for all individuals, still there is no soul to whom it does not in some way speak of the goodness and beauty of the Lord.

"For how great is His goodness, and how great is His beauty." Let those words be the point of departure for your private worship today.

JUNE 28

They rehearsed all that God had done with them, and how He had opened the door of faith unto the Gentiles (Acts 14:27).

There never was a briefer report of a more important piece of service than that given in this verse. Paul and Barnabas have returned from their first missionary journey. With great courage they have preached the Gospel in Cyprus, Antioch of Pisidia, Iconium, Derbe, and Lystra. God has mightily blessed their testimony and has preserved them even from death. Now they are back at Antioch reporting to the Church. Notice the two elements of that report. 1. "They rehearsed all that *God* had done with them." 2. "How *He* had opened the door of faith unto the Gentiles." The emphasis is completely on God. If ever men had thrilling exploits of which to boast Paul and Barnabas had. But they were scrupulous in recognizing that everything they accomplished was of God.

When men have this attitude toward Christian work, when they get to the point of caring nothing for personal praise but giving *all* the glory to God, then they may be used as Paul and Barnabas were used. Self-glory is the enemy of spiritual power; giving God the glory is the pathway to blessing.

JUNE 29

There was a man sent from God, whose name was John (John 1: 6).

No higher thing can be said of anyone. But have you ever stopped to think that John the Baptist is not the only one of whom it might be said? It might even apply to you and me. God has a work for every Christian to do; for each of us He has our appointed task to which He sends us and us alone. The glory of John the Baptist lay in his complete submission to the divine commission. Many are sent but few really go! John was not only sent from God; he also went for God. Had he failed in his going, the fact of his sending would never have been recorded.

JUNE 30

Abide in Me, and I in you (John 15: 4).

In this short sentence lies the secret of the Christian life. To begin to comprehend that secret it is necessary to know what the Lord Jesus meant by the word "abide." He took the familiar word for "remain" and put into it great depths of meaning, so that it signifies a living, organic union. Those who are truly abiding in Christ are thus, as Thayer puts it, "knit to Him by the Spirit they have received from Him." He is the root of their innermost lives: from Him they are continually, consciously and unconsciously, drawing their spiritual sustenance.

Abiding in Christ is a simple thing; but, like so many of the simple things of our Lord's teaching, it has inexhaustible depths of meaning. It begins and continues with faith, the faith of committal that by an act of the will rests wholly upon Christ. Everything, therefore, that savors of self-will apart from Christ is contrary to abiding. Even when the believer, is engaged in earthly affairs, his soul may unconsciously abide in Christ, just as we have our homes, although we do not constantly think of the fact that we live in them.

Notice finally that our Lord uses the imperative. "Abide in Me," is His command. What a blessing will result if we make it our spiritual business daily to learn more of what it means to abide in Christ!

JULY 1

And holiness, without which no man shall see the Lord (Heb. 12:14).

Let these words remind us of the uniqueness of holiness. There are many virtues, but holiness is the only one of them that evil men cannot share. It is possible for a bad man to be courageous, or unselfish, kind, or even loving. He may mix truthfulness and justice with his evil. But he can never be holy. Of all the virtues, holiness is the most divine. And it is the possession of the regenerate alone. No man is naturally holy; by nature all are sinners. Our hope of holiness is in Christ alone. Only through our second birth by faith in Him can we see God. Oh, that more of us Christians would really "take time to be holy."

JULY 2

But even unto this day, when Moses is read, the vail is upon their heart. Nevertheless when it shall turn to the Lord, the vail shall be taken away (II Cor. 3:15, 16).

While the obvious reference in these two verses is to the judicial blindness of Israel, we may see in them a spiritual truth applying to all of us. "Nevertheless when it (the heart) shall turn to the Lord the vail (of unbelief) shall be taken away." Now in verse 14, Paul has written of Israel that "their minds were blinded." But the remedy for this blindness, yes, even blindness of the mind in spiritual things is a heart matter, for in verse 16 the apostle says, "When it [by which he refers to the heart as mentioned in verse 16] shall turn to the Lord, the vail shall be taken away."

What do we learn by this? We learn that spiritual enlightenment comes in the first instance only when the heart turns to the Lord. It is a dangerous thing to decry the place of true emotion in religion, for when the heart is right with God, the mind is bound to follow suit. Surely it is significant that the most intellectual of the apostles acknowledges so plainly the heart turned Christ-ward as the source of spiritual illumination.

Would we see clearly in all the moral and spiritual issues of our lives? Then we must make sure that our hearts are daily turned to the Lord Jesus.

JULY 3

The God that answereth by fire, let Him be God (I Kings 18: 24).

Fire represents the essential element of judgment in God's nature. And there come times when God must vindicate Himself by fire. For there are some things He can answer only by judgment. That this age is rapidly heading toward such a time few thoughtful Christians will deny. So great is the mass of accumulated wickedness that the divine fire of judgment will alone suffice to deal with it.

As more of God's people realize this fact, a greater urgency will come into their witness. Days of such moment as these are no time for trifling. The one message of shelter through the Lamb of God must be proclaimed everywhere. Secondary emphases must be put aside, while salvation through Christ is heralded to a world fast heading for the fire of God's final judgment.

JULY 4

And they stood up in their place, and read in the book of the law of the Lord their God one fourth part of the day; and another fourth part they confessed, and worshipped the Lord their God (Neh. 9:3).

The setting of this verse goes back to B.C. 445 when a fast was celebrated after the rebuilding of the wall of Jerusalem. And, as the record states, that fast day was carefully divided into reading the Word of God, confession, and worship. The example is one that, if followed more generally, would lead to a sounder type of Christian living. Reading the Bible is essential, but by itself it is not enough for the soul's best welfare. Prayer, of which confession is a part, is absolutely necessary, but prayer alone does not make a rounded spiritual life. Similarly worship in public as well as private is indispensable, but it too is not enough. Reading the Word of God nourishes the soul and imparts God's will to the believer; prayer and confession bring him into close communion with God; worship honours and praises the God Who is revealed in Scripture and Who hears and answers prayer.

Christian friend, is your spiritual life a balanced one? Are you really taking time for the Bible, for prayer and confession, and for worship?

JULY 5

There is no fear in love; but perfect love casteth out fear: because fear hath torment. He that feareth is not made perfect in love (I John 4:18).

It will reward us today to look with a special care at one word in this verse of marvelous reassurance. "Perfect love," says John, "casteth out fear." What then does he mean by "*perfect* love"? Well, John uses the word *teleia* for perfect. And the more common meaning of *teleia* is finished; it definitely applies to that which has reached its end or goal. With this in mind, we are warranted in reaching an important conclusion. The kind of love to which John refers is the love that has reached its goal, and the goal of love for us Christians is none other than a Person, even the Lord Jesus Christ. So long as our love is truly set on Him, so long as it rests in its goal in Christ, fear can have no power over us.

JULY 6

Thou art my hiding place; Thou shalt preserve me from trouble; Thou shalt compass me about with songs of deliverance. Selah (Ps. 32:7).

Our meditation upon this heartening verse may be summed up in one word thrice repeated—"Thou—Thou—Thou." As David found in God peace amid trouble, so have all believers through the years fled to the Rock of Ages. When trial and sorrow come into our lives and the enemy presses hard upon us, we naturally flee to some hiding place. Our first impulse is to find a deliverer and to seek a shelter in the storm. And it is emphatically true that just any hiding place, or any deliverer, or any shelter is not sufficient. The storms that beset us are fierce storms, the enemy who attacks is a powerful enemy. Just any refuge will not do. And so we learn like David that the only safe refuge is God. If, in answer to God's question as to our hiding place, we can say "Thou"; if we can claim Him alone as our divine Preserver in trouble; if we find in Him our Deliverer Who compasses us about, we shall indeed stand fast in the evil day.

JULY 7

Our Lord Jesus Christ, Who gave Himself for our sins, that He might deliver us from this present evil world, according to the will of God and our Father (Gal. 1:3,4).

These magnificent words, so packed with meaning, occur in the salutation of the letter. Mark how clearly they state the reason for Christ's death—"that He might deliver us from this present evil world." That is what He has actually done for us. In our position before God, in the destiny of our souls, we are completely delivered. But, O Christian, *where* are you actually living? The Israelites were truly delivered from Egypt, but they longed to go back there. And in their sinful desires and their practices they really did go back to Egypt. Oh, child of God, for whose redemption from "this present evil world" Christ paid the price of His blood, do not go back to that world either in word, thought or deed!

JULY 8

A man can receive nothing, except it be given him from Heaven (John 3:27).

By this one sentence pride is outlawed. If everything a man has is a gift from God, then there is no place for human pride in anything. What is pride? Well, it is the sin that cheats by robbing God of the glory. We may, for instance, take legitimate pleasure in the exercise of some special ability God has given us; but the sin of pride lies in our taking personal credit for that thing. Pride is at bottom intensely and egotistically possessive. It says of its object, "This is mine and mine alone. Therefore this glorifies me and me alone." It is compounded of lying, for the thing of which we are proud comes from God only; it is compounded of theft, for it steals the praise that belongs to God alone; and it is complicated by base ingratitude, for it ignores the Giver.

Oh, that everyone of us Christians may give God the glory in all things! "A man can receive nothing, except it be given him from Heaven."

JULY 9

Worthy of death (Rom. 1:32).

Sometime when you are alone with God take your Bible
and mark these three words. Then go back over verses 29-31
and encircle lightly with a pencil (you will probably want to
erase later) every sin that is present or has ever been present
in your life. Now draw lines connecting those circles to the
phrase "worthy of death," and you will see why Christ had
to die for you. Doubtless there will be some sins like murder
that you will not have to encircle. But there will be plenty
of others that you cannot evade; perhaps envy, or whispering
(gossip), or pride, or disobedience will be among them. God's
verdict upon each of these is the same as His verdict upon
murder. Sin, even in its more refined forms, is a capital
crime, and God demands its capital punishment. "Worthy of
death." Yes, respectable church-member, that is what God
says of you. That is why Christ died—to take upon Himself
the death-penalty that is yours. Oh, the wonder of redeeming
love!

JULY 10

For the people had a mind to work (Neh. 4:6).

Within the short space of fifty-two days Nehemiah pushed
through the building of the wall of Jerusalem. And he did
it in the face of the bitter, sly, and resourceful opposition
of Sanballat and Tobiah. It was a great feat, and one of
the secrets of its success is found in our text for today, "For
the people had a mind to work."

The application is plain. Christ's Church is saved by grace;
faith, not works, is the basis of its redemption. But how
necessary it is for that Church to "have a mind to work" for
Him Who wrought our salvation upon the accursed tree. Paul
had such a mind; so did Luther, and Calvin, and Wesley, and
Livingstone, and Hudson Taylor, and Moody. Do you, Christian friend, really have "a mind to work" for God? The
Lord's power is unlimited, and no man knows what or how
much He can do through even a small group of His children
who are actually determined to work for Him.

JULY 11

Come unto Me, all ye that labour and are heavy laden, and I will give you rest. Take My yoke upon you . . . (Matt. 11: 28, 29).

There is a profound paradox in these precious words. "Rest" and "yoke"—the two seem diametrically opposed. For a yoke implies active work, while rest implies quietness. And the Lord is in effect saying to those who are worn out with toil and bowed beneath their burdens, "I will give you rest by setting you to work under a yoke." Yet in these very words He enunciates a great principle of the human spirit. True rest, He is teaching, lies in the right kind of work. And the right kind of work is any work shared with Him. With His yoke upon us, with Him at our side, our work turns into rest, even rest in our very soul. Thus we learn that rest is not just cessation of work. It is rather labor done under the easy yoke of Christ. For that yoke transforms the hardest toil into joyful recreation of soul.

JULY 12

The Lord looseth the prisoners (Ps. 146:7).

What a far-reaching work that is! Everywhere human life is in bondage. Men and women are prisoners of disease and ignorance, of habit and fear, of worry and depression, and, most of all, of sin. Millions today need political liberty, but more millions need spiritual emancipation. The most precious freedom is that of the soul, and only Christ gives it. In His first recorded message, delivered in the synagogue at Nazareth, the Lord Jesus preached from Isaiah 61:1, in which occurs these words: "The Spirit of the Lord God is upon Me, because He hath anointed Me . . . to preach deliverance to the captives."

He Whom the Psalmist saw through distant prophecy lived and taught and died and rose for us. The perfect freedom of His love is now ours through faith. What folly, therefore, for any of us to sell our birthright of inner liberty for a pottage of anxious care, binding habit, or downright sin! "The Lord looses the prisoners." If you are in bondage to anything at all, let Christ make you free.

JULY 13

Commit thy works unto the Lord, and thy thoughts shall be established (Prov. 16: 3).

There are two main ideas in this verse and their relation is that of cause and effect. The principle set forth is a very practical one. Indeed it may be well called a sure cure for worry. The marginal reading suggests that the meaning of the word *commit* is "roll." When we learn to *roll* all our ways and works upon the Lord, we shall have the peace that comes from a mind which is established in Him. But if we insist on bearing every burden ourselves, we cannot expect to enjoy that quietness of mind which is the prerogative of the life staid on Him.

JULY 14

Believest thou this? (John 11: 26).

The Lord Jesus asks the question. He is speaking to Martha, who is grieving for her brother, Lazarus, and He has just made that glorious declaration of Christian hope: "I am the resurrection and the life; he that believeth in Me, though he were dead, yet shall he live: and whosoever liveth and believeth in Me shall never die."

Now there is a world of meaning in this question that our Lord asked troubled Martha. He did not say to her, "Understandest thou this?" Had He done that, He would have cut off not only Martha but all humanity from the hope that is in Himself. For no man can understand the mystery of the resurrection. Nor can any man understand fully the other great Christian doctrines. And so Christ never demands intellectual understanding of spiritual things. But He does ask for faith that is childlike enough to believe what it cannot understand.

Why did Martha reply, "Yea, Lord: I believe . . ."? She believed, not because she understood Christ's words, but because she knew Christ. Out of her personal knowledge of Him grew the confidence that led her to believe that her dead brother would rise. Is it not the same with us? We believe what we cannot understand, because we know that Christ is trustworthy. It is a law of spiritual living that the more we are in fellowship with the Lord Jesus and the better we know Him, the more fully we believe His words.

JULY 15

My brethren, count it all joy whon yo fall into divero temptations (James 1: 2).

A freer translation of this verse reinforces its inspiring message. "My brethren," James is saying, "count it a thing wholly joyful whenever you fall into manifold trials." Inspiring counsel indeed, but how few of us heed it! There come trials in our lives. How prone we are to bewail them! "Oh," we cry, "I have this difficult problem. I face this trying interview. I must meet this unjust accusation." But that is not the attitude the Word of God, as it comes to us through James, would have us take. The Word of God would have us rejoice, even to the extent of finding a zest in facing our difficulties. Why? Because we ourselves are able to overcome them? No, but because Christ is Victor and our extremities are His opportunities to triumph gloriously.

JULY 16

I exhort therefore, that, first of all, supplications, prayers, intercessions, and giving of thanks, be made for all men; for kings, and for all that are in authority (I Tim. 2:1, 2).

We see in these words from the longest of the pastoral epistles the first duty of a Christian church. "First of all," prayer (and the apostle lists no less than four different kinds of prayer) is to be made for all men; and then Paul specifically states that kings and all in authority are to be particularly mentioned by the church. What a timely exhortation that is! And what a difficult one! Notice that Paul makes absolutely no distinction between good and bad rulers. Had he desired to differentiate between the two, he might well have excepted tyrants, for he lived under the rule of Nero.

It takes a large-hearted pastor and a truly Christian church to obey this primary exhortation, when feeling is running high and hate is swelling in many a heart. But God commands that all are to be prayed for, enemies as well as friends, aggressors as well as the innocently afflicted. For all men have souls, and Christ died for the wicked. It may be hard to pray for a dreaded dictator, for instance, but it is nevertheless Christian to supplicate God to touch his heart and lead him to salvation.

JULY 17

*And I will walk among you, and will be your God, and ye
shall be My people* (Lev. 26:12).

On the authority of Paul in II Corinthians 6:16, we Christians may claim this wonderful promise. Paul applies it to
the life of the believer. We are, he is saying, God's temple,
for God has said, "I will dwell in them, and walk in them."
Therefore, we cannot have too high a conception of the
spiritual life. When we grasp the fact that the Christian
life is the life of God living in us and walking in us, then
we shall be more careful of what we do and where we go,
what we read, what we see, and what we think. When we
realize Who it is Who indwells us, then we shall really want
to separate ourselves from worldliness.

JULY 18

*For thus saith the Lord God, the Holy One of Israel; In re-
turning and rest shall ye be saved; in quietness and in confidence shall be your strength: and ye would not* (Isa. 30:15).

It was in the face of impending invasion by Sennacherib,
King of Assyria, that the prophet gave this beautiful word to
God's people. And now, millenniums after the Assyrian empire has crumbled to dust, the promise still stands. Its endurance results from the fact that in it God expressed the
root principle of salvation. The emphasis is not upon man's
action, but upon man's reliance upon God. Salvation, says
the prophet, lies in returning and rest; strength comes from
quietness and confidence. Thus it is in every age. As we
turn to the Lord in complete reliance, we learn to know the
fuller meaning of our salvation. When we cease to bustle
about in self-activity, and rest in quietness and confidence,
we begin to appropriate something of the strength of our
Heavenly Father.

But how sad are these last words of the verse, "And ye
would not!" May God never point to one of His promises
and say of our failure to rely upon it, "Ye would not!"

JULY 19

O that one might plead for a man with God, as a man pleadeth for his neighbor (Job 16: 21).

This exalted wish of Job's has literally come true. A man may now plead with God for his friend. The Lord Jesus has made us believers "kings and priests unto Him." And the office of a priest is to intercede. Yes, what Job longed for is a reality. Men may come boldly unto the Throne of Grace there to plead for their friends. The vail has been rent; the privilege of intercession is open for every believer. But, Christian friend, how are you exercising your priestly prerogative? Do you know what it is to go into the Lord's presence, burdened not for yourself and your own needs, but for someone else? Have you ever wrestled with God that your friend might obtain a blessing?

JULY 20

And David said, Is there yet any that is left of the house of Saul, that I may show him kindness for Jonathan's sake? (II Sam. 9:1).

In the annals of David's reign the story of Mephibosheth is an interlude of striking beauty that stands as one of the most remarkable foreshadowings of Gospel grace in all the Old Testament. David and Jonathan had made their famous love-covenant. Jonathan had died in battle, David was upon the throne, but the covenant was not forgotten. It outlasted Jonathan's death; and so we find David inquiring for some remnant of the house of Saul that he might show him favor for his friend's sake. Just how earnest was David's search is witnessed by his searching out Ziba (vs. 2) and through his finding Mephibosheth (vss. 3-5).

"That I might show him kindness for Jonathan's sake." Verily, that is of the precious essence of grace. It was not that Mephibosheth in himself merited kindness; there was nothing in him to deserve the king's favor. But because of another, even Jonathan, the king was eager to bless him. Just so we sinners are God's Mephibosheths. Without merit in ourselves, we yet are found of His Love and blessed beyond all our deserts for Christ's sake.

JULY 21

Now when Mephibosheth, the son of Jonathan, the son of Saul, was come unto David, he fell on his face, and did reverence (II Sam. 9:6).

Mephibosheth was lame and therefore, according to the estimate of those war-like times in which he lived, quite worthless. But God gave him an enduring testimony through the quiet example of his life. For Mephibosheth will ever be remembered for the manner in which he received the grace that was shown him. Realizing his own lack of worth, he made no pretense of meriting any claim upon David's favor. So, coming into this king's presence, he simply fell on his face and did reverence. And then, in answer to the king's greeting, he replied, "Behold, thy servant!"

Oh, if more of us could realize that we are at best quite weak and worthless in ourselves, we should please our Lord more by adopting the Mephibosheth attitude. Let us remember that a holy God owes no sinner anything; He has been under no obligation to save a single soul. Thus, if we have heard Him call us by name unto the eternal blessedness of salvation, can we do less than did Mephibosheth when David called him by name—can we do less than respond out of hearts full of humble reverence, "Behold thy servant"?

JULY 22

As for Mephibosheth, said the king, he shall eat at my table, as one of the king's sons (II Sam. 9:11).

Here we have illustrated the length to which God goes in His sovereign grace. He takes the worthless sinner and not only blesses him but brings him into His own family as a son, a relationship that the New Testament epistles call "the adoption of sons." How marvelous! The erstwhile stranger from the kingdom, alienated because of his sin, is lifted up into a family relationship with the King of kings!

If our religious life today is shallow, it is because so many have yet to apprehend these great doctrines of sin and grace. The greatest need in religious life today is not more activity, but more of the kind of meditation upon the truth of our redemption that drives the soul's roots deep down into the grace of God.

JULY 23

But the king spared Mephibosheth . . . because of the Lord's oath that was between them, between David and Jonathan (II Sam. 21:7).

Here, set like a jewel in this stern and bloody story, is another reminder of the long memory of grace. It was in David's youth that he had made his love-covenant with Jonathan. And now, long years after Jonathan's death, and years after Mephibosheth had been taken into David's household, a threat arises against Mephibosheth's life. A descendant of Saul, he is liable to execution as an atonement for Saul's violation of the ancient treaty with the Gibeonites. But the sentence of death passes over Mephibosheth, because David in his sovereign power and out of his undying love for Jonathan, wills to do so.

Our spiritual imagination is weak indeed if we fail to see in all this the comforting truth that those who are under grace are forever safe. The old covenant with the Gibeonites could not disturb Mephibosheth's security. No more can anything in Heaven or on earth bring into condemnation a soul that is trusting Christ for salvation. To be under grace is to be secure forever.

JULY 24

. . . those that remember His commandments to do them (Ps. 103:18).

Thus does the Psalmist describe those who receive the everlasting mercy of the Lord and His righteousness. They remember God's commandments, he says, with the result that they do them. In their case the Word of God leads to action. They not only hear the commandments; they store them in their memories. But they store them in their memories for the purpose of doing them. Behind all of God's blessings is the simple principle of obedience. It is not the keeping of commandments that makes us children of God, but after we are saved by grace our blessing depends in large measure upon our obedience to the revealed will of our blessed Lord. Oh, for more Christians who will consistently remember His commandments *to do them*!

JULY 25

He could not be hid (Mark 7: 24).

It was in the Gentile regions of Tyre and Sidon that the Lord Jesus entered into a house, "but He could not be hid." Today He awaits us at the right hand of God, but His Holy Spirit is here on earth dwelling in every single person who has been born again. The Spirit of Christ enters our hearts the moment we are saved. Are we hiding the indwelling Christ? Jesus could not be hid in the borders of Tyre and Sidon. That is a historical fact. But is He hid in your life, covered over by worldliness, obscured by evil habits and besetting sin? Are you hiding your divine Guest, so that no one knows He dwells with you, so that you are powerless to bring spiritual help to the perishing? God grant that we may be so transparent that all may see Christ in us, the hope of glory!

JULY 26

He trusted in the Lord God of Israel (II Kings 18:5).

There are lessons to be learned from the records of great men. When God gives a particularly full account of a man's life and work, as He has done in the case of King Hezekiah, we may be sure that He has something to teach us from that life.

The two books of Kings are in the main a record of human failure. Time after time we find a king's reign summed up in some such words as these: "He did that which was evil in the sight of the Lord." But there are a few exceptions, and Hezekiah is outstanding among them. Let us understand from our verse for today that God has His summary of every life. In the case of Hezekiah, it took the form of highest commendation. And the reason for this is not far to seek. "He trusted," says the record, "in the Lord God of Israel." Notice that there was nothing peculiar to royalty in that. You do not have to be a king or queen to trust God. Any Christian, however humble his circumstances, may lay the same foundation for a life well-pleasing to God that Hezekiah laid.

Suppose your life were soon to end. Could God begin His estimate of it by saying of you, "He trusted"?

JULY 27

But as touching the resurrection of the dead, have ye not read that which was spoken unto you by God? (Matt. 22:31).

"Have you read," the Lord Jesus asked the unbelieving Sadducees, "that which was spoken unto *you* by God?" Notice the amazing implication of that word "you." The very next verse cites words that God spoke to Moses (Exod. 3:6). Yet here Christ expressly challenges the Sadducees on the ground that God's statement to Moses was also addressed to them. Could there be a clearer evidence of our Lord's use of Scripture as a message for all men in all times? When God spoke to Moses, He spoke also to the Sadducees and to us as well. And when the Lord Jesus spoke to the Sadducees or to the disciples, He spoke to you and to me. The amazing vitality of the Word of God lies in the fact that it is a personal message to every man from Almighty God.

JULY 28

Avoid shameful and foolish talk and low jesting—they are all alike discreditable and in place of these give thanks (Eph. 5:4, Weymouth).

Three verbal vices are warned against in this exhortation. Let us pay some attention to the third. The Authorized Version calls it merely "jesting," and thereby causes some solemn people to think that the apostle is attacking legitimate humor. But the word has nothing to do with wholesome fun and harmless joking. The Greek illumines itself. As Dr. Vincent points out, it is a compound of *eu* (meaning "well") and *trepo* (meaning "to turn"). It therefore describes the manner of speech which adapts itself too readily to its surroundings. It may be a very witty and polished way of talking but it has no principles. When sacred things are flouted, it chimes in; when impurity prevails, it goes along; when false accusation is made, it lifts no opposing voice. All too characteristic of many in the church today, it purchases urbanity and popularity at the expense of conscience. Let us avoid it like the verbal poison that it is.

JULY 29

Pray with unceasing prayer and entreaty at all times in the Spirit, and be always on the alert to seize opportunities for doing so (Eph. 6:18, Weymouth).

Oh, the missed opportunities for prayer in our lives! For example when awakening at night, when waiting for an appointment, or when traveling and time hangs heavy on our hands—in all these we have opportunities for prayer. How was it that Paul, the writer of great epistles, the evangelizer of an empire, and the one upon whom the care of all the churches came daily, maintained his fervent prayer-life? Only by being, as he exhorts us in this Ephesian letter, "Always on the alert to seize opportunities for prayer."

The next time you are wakeful at night or are kept waiting for an appointment, be on the alert to seize that opportunity for prayer. And use it for intercession in bringing to the throne of grace some one in special need. It may be some missionary in a difficult place, or some friend or relative in great trial. Your prayer will help.

JULY 30

When Jesus then lifted up His eyes, and saw a great company come unto Him, He saith unto Philip . . . (John 6:5).

There was a great problem; 5,000 people had to be fed. There is much instruction for us in the manner in which that problem was solved. As Luke tells us, the Lord Jesus said, "Make them sit down by fifties in a company." We may take this as typical of the fact that the problem was faced squarely and frankly. Again, notice that those 5,000 were a mixed multitude. Nevertheless, those in charge were willing to give the control over the situation to Christ. And with Him in control the problem was solved; the 5,000 were fed. There was no need for agonizing, no frantic pleading. There was simply on His part an honest recognition of the problem, a calm looking to the Father, and the inevitable solution. Christian friend, that formula is still valid and will solve your problems and mine. Face your difficulty, give the Lord Jesus control, look in calm faith to Him, and He *will* deal with the matter.

JULY 31

He that believeth on Me, as the Scripture hath said, from within him shall flow rivers of living water (John 7: 38, A. S. V.).

Let us just take this verse at its face value as a plain statement of fact regarding all who believe on Christ. Such persons, Christ says, shall have within them springs of living water. The salvation they possess will flow out in abundant streams.

You are a believer. But is John 7:38 true of you? Is the water of life actually issuing from your heart? "This spake He of the Spirit," says the next verse, thereby defining the living water as coming from the indwelling Spirit of Christ. No living spring can be confined without an outlet; nor can the Spirit of the living Christ be locked up in the human breast. If the life-giving truth is not issuing from you, you may well begin to inquire whether you have the Holy Spirit within you.

"But," someone says, "how may I have the Holy Spirit?" By faith. That is the Scriptural answer. "He that *believeth* on Me," said the Lord Jesus, "from within him shall flow rivers of living waters." And if there are some who lack those living waters, let them go back and examine the nature and extent of their belief. Many adherents of evangelical Christianity fail because they have an all too shallow conception of what it means to believe on Christ. Complete turning from self and full committal of the soul to the Lord Jesus as Saviour never fails to bring to a heart and life the life-giving and life-producing power of the Holy Spirit.

Spirit of God, descend upon my heart;
Wean it from earth; through all its pulses move;
Stoop to my weakness mighty as Thou art,
And make me love Thee as I ought to love.

AUGUST 1

Jesus of Nazareth . . . Who went about doing good, and healing all that were oppressed of the devil (Acts 10:38).

Christ is our pattern, but, as we clearly see from this verse, there are some things in which we cannot follow Him. We can all go about doing good, but we cannot all do the miracles He did. How strong the obligation, then, to follow Him to the limit of our capacity! The gift of healing seems to have been conferred on only a select few of the disciples, but the ability to do good is universally distributed. Beware of looking at Christ's unique miracles and saying, "I can't follow Him; I can't give sight to the blind, multiply the loaves, raise the dead and heal the possessed." God never called you to follow Christ a step beyond your own capacity. Do not forget that Christ "went about doing good." When you do likewise, directed by His Spirit, you are as truly following Him as if you were performing some spectacular miracle.

AUGUST 2

. . . Barnabas and Paul, men that have hazarded their lives for the Name of our Lord Jesus Christ (Acts 15:25, 26).

These words are from the decision of James at the first Church Council at Jerusalem. What a marvelous recommendation they are of Paul and Barnabas!

How many of us Christians of a latter day could be characterized in similar terms? "Oh," you reply, "I have never had an opportunity to hazard my life for the Lord Jesus." Nevertheless, there should reside in you the very spirit of Paul and Barnabas, that will risk, if needs be, your life for Christ. You may be certain of this one thing: if you are not able to stand ridicule and misunderstanding and disappointment for the sake of Christ, you can hardly expect, if the test comes, to risk your life for his sake. Those who do not know what it means to martyr their pride and self-indulgence are not made of the stuff of which Paul and Barnabas were made. The present hazarding of your life means the daily mortification of your own selfish will.

AUGUST 3

And there was very great gladness (Neh. 8:17).

This comment comes at the close of the account of the restoration of the Feast of Tabernacles by the Jews who, under Nehemiah's leadership, had returned to Jerusalem from captivity. The law had been read and explained to all the people by Ezra. But that was not all. Having heard the law, the people obeyed it. "And there was," says the record, "very great gladness."

We see, therefore, that obedience brings gladness. One way in which we experience the joy of the Lord is through obeying Him. You and I are not called upon to keep the Feast of Tabernacles, but God does have His will for us. When we obey that will, then we experience a gladness and joy which no worldly pleasure can ever rival.

AUGUST 4

I and My Father are One (John 10:30).

So tremendous is this statement and such violent opposition did it call forth that our attention is likely to be diverted from its immediate connection. Our Lord has been emphasizing a very comforting truth; He has been speaking (vss. 25-29) of His relationship to His sheep who, He says, "shall never perish," because "no man is able to pluck them out of My hand." And then He makes this stupendous self-disclosure, "I and My Father are One." This is the climax of His teaching about His relationship to His sheep, the crowning guarantee of their eternal security. Were Christ anything less than God, there might be some doubt as to the security of His own. For only divine omnipotence can give promise of complete and everlasting safety. But because Christ is God, He is able to take perfect care of His sheep. Therefore let us rejoice that He Who is our Shepherd-Saviour is He Who could truly say, "I and My Father are One." When fear besets us and our faith falters, let us just rest in the assurance that the Lord Almighty is our Shepherd Lord.

AUGUST 5

For the ways of man are before . . . the Lord, and He pondereth all his goings (Prov. 5:21).

It is a startling thought that God gives more careful consideration to the average life than the possessor of that life. Men are so prone to carelessness. They drift along from day to day, giving little thought either to the way in which they are going or to their ultimate destiny. Some few may think earnestly about their lives, but very many just let themselves be borne along by the current. But God *considers* our doings. What we do means something to Him. The Maker and Ruler of all things *ponders* our lives. What an incentive for more holy living!

AUGUST 6

Be anxious for nothing; but in everything with prayer and thanksgiving let your requests be made known unto God. And the peace of God which passeth all understanding shall keep your hearts and minds through Christ Jesus (Phil. 4: 6, 7).

The vitally important thing for us to remember regarding these two verses is the logical relationship of cause and effect in which they stand. When we come to the place of giving up anxiety, then it follows as the night the day that God gives us His peace.

Have you ever thought deeply about the surpassing value of the peace of God? Have you seen clearly that it is an active thing, divinely appointed to render you a definite servise; that it is given, as Weymouth translates it, to "be a garrison to guard your hearts and minds in Christ Jesus?" When you and I begin to understand the matchless worth of the peace of God, we shall be more ready to do the thing necessary to receive it, which is to give up anxiety.

But let us never say, "Yes, I know Scripture tells us to be anxious for nothing, but after all there are some things we just can't help worrying about." Whenever we talk like that, we are violating the spiritual logic whereby God confers His peace. Let us remember that the command not to worry admits of no exceptions.

AUGUST 7

False teachers . . . denying the Lord that bought them . . . many shall follow their pernicious ways (II Peter 2:1, 2).

Among the most severe portions in the New Testament is this second chapter of II Peter. It stands with Jude as a burning denunciation of apostasy. As one reads it over in its entirety, he is impressed with the fact that apostasy, beginning with denial of the truth as to the Person of Christ, finally and inevitably manifests itself in wrong life.

We see, therefore, that there is a direct relationship between what a man believes or denies and what he is. If we want to know how much of the Gospel we actually believe, we can answer the question by inquiring how much of the truth we are living. We say that we believe in God; but do we worry? We affirm our belief in Christ; but are we really abiding in Him? We testify to our belief in prayer; but are we actually going in secret every day before the Throne of Grace?

AUGUST 8

Forgetting those things which are behind, and reaching forth unto those things which are before, I press toward the mark for the prize of the high calling (Phil. 3:13, 14).

The backward look in Christian living is very dangerous. Harping on forgiven sins dishonors the God of all mercy Who has expressly said of His people, "I will remember their sin no more." Surely one of the favorite devices of the adversary is to tempt us Christians to worry over past difficulties. How senseless! All the fretting and worry in the world cannot change a single thing that has happened. And after all, if we are now dwelling in the love of Christ, how can anything past possibly alienate us from Him?

That Paul was alive to this danger of the backward look is made vividly clear in these great words. Oh, if all who read them would forget the mistakes and transgressions of yesterday and, with their eyes fixed upon the Lord Jesus, press on toward Him, there would be fewer failures today! Are you trusting Christ enough to leave the past to Him?

AUGUST 9

For He remembered His holy promise, and Abraham His servant (Ps. 105: 42).

This statement follows a long list of the Lord's miraculous interventions in Israel's behalf, the plagues of Egypt, the cloud and the pillar of fire, the quails, and the water from the rock being among them. And then, in these few words, the reason behind these miracles is given. It is simply that the Lord *remembered* His promises and Abraham His servant. Why Abraham? Because Abraham was the father of Israel and the promises were made first to Him. So every Christian should look back upon God's dealings with him and say, out of his own life, "He has remembered His holy promises, and Christ His Son." For the Lord indeed remembers His promises. That is why they never wear out. A single verse of Scripture may be used a thousand times and remain as new and comforting as when its truth was first realized in your heart and applied in your life.

AUGUST 10

And thou shalt make a plate of pure gold, and grave upon it . . . HOLINESS TO THE LORD . . . and it shall be upon Aaron's forehead (Exod. 28:36-38).

It is significant that the plate of pure gold, saying *holiness to the Lord*, was placed on the high priest's forehead. The suggestion is plainly that the mind must be set apart to God. Surely if Aaron were holy in his thoughts, he would be holy in his deeds.

Long ago the Hebrew priesthood was abrogated, but it has its wider succession today in the priesthood of the Christian believer. Peter writes, "Ye are . . . a royal priesthood" (I Peter 2:9); and John says that the Lord Jesus "has made us kings and priests unto God" (Rev. 1:6). Yes, Christian believer, *you* are a priest unto God. But is *holiness to the Lord* written across *your* forehead? Are you consciously seeking by faith to bring "into captivity every thought to the obedience of Christ" (II Cor. 10:5)? Make no mistake; you will never live a holy life until you learn to think holy thoughts.

AUGUST 11

And they overcame him by the blood of the Lamb, and by the word of their testimony (Rev. 12:11).

There is a sense in which testimony is a powerful weapon for overcoming the devil. A believer who testifies constantly becomes irrevocably committed to Christ's cause. Certain avenues that lead to sin, certain associations that would defile, are closed to him by the word of his testimony. And as he continues his testimony, his own hold on divine truth is strengthened. Indeed, it is extremely doubtful whether the overcoming life can be lived apart from definite witness. While the victory is in the first instance already won through the blood of the Lamb, the believer's grasp of victory is strengthened through his testimony.

AUGUST 12

The Lord is a God of judgment: blessed are all they that wait for Him (Isa. 30:18).

And the Lord God remains a God of judgment! But let all of us who trust in Him remember that He cannot be hurried. There is a difference between the delays of men and the delays of God. Man, because of weakness, or fear, or ignorance, may be slow in administering justice, even to the extent of neglecting it altogether. God sometimes delays, but always for His all-wise purpose. And, wherever judgment is demanded, God is certain to consummate it. For Him to leave one single injustice eternally unsettled is impossible. The darker the days, the more firmly must we cling to the fact that God will never fail to right every wrong. But He acts in His own time. Our part is patient waiting. To wait for God to vindicate His justice is a sure gateway to spiritual blessedness. "The Lord is a God of judgment"—that is the unshakable assurance of His ultimately prevailing justice. "Blessed are all they that wait for Him"—that is the beatitude for sorely tried believers who, in spite of every calamity, are holding fast their faith in the justice of God.

AUGUST 13

*And He had in His right hand seven stars . . . and when
I saw Him, I fell at His feet as dead. And He laid His right
hand upon me, saying unto me, Fear not . . .* (Rev. 1:16, 17).

These words from John's inspired picture of the risen
Christ bring us a message of comfort regarding the right hand
of our Lord. In John's vision of Christ that hand held the
seven stars, but, when John "fell at His feet as dead,"
Christ laid His right hand upon him and said, "Fear not."

Do you not see the comforting principle? The hand which
upholds all things is yet the hand that reaches down to you
and says, no matter what your circumstances may be, "Fear
not." Christ's hand of power is the hand of reassurance.

AUGUST 14

If any man thirst, let him come unto Me, and drink (John
7:37).

It was in the last day of the Feast of Tabernacles that the
Lord Jesus stood and cried out this invitation. The invitation
still stands. Since the day He uttered it, nothing has happened to revoke it. Christ is always ready to quench the
thirst of every dry and parched soul. The water of life is
available "without money and without price." What wealth
cannot purchase, thirst procures. Any man, anywhere, at
any time may have his soul refreshed in Christ.

Yet there is a strange thing about this invitation. It is
both universal and limited. It is universal because it applies
to all men. It is limited because only those who are thirsty
are capable of responding to it. By nature all men are in
a state of spiritual aridness, for all men need Christ. But
only those who are awake to their dryness to the extent of
thirsting for Him, will come to Christ for the life-giving
water He alone can give. "Blessed are they," said our Lord,
"who . . . thirst after righteousness, for they shall be filled."
It is a great thing to develop your sense of spiritual thirst,
for it is your thirst that will drive you straight to Him Who
alone gives the water of life freely.

AUGUST 15

Thou renderest to every man according to his work (Ps. 62:12).

God makes no exceptions. Every man means *every* man. Saint and sinner are dealt with according to their individual work. To be sure, the saint is in Heaven solely through God's grace; yet there before the Presence of Christ his works are to be judged. And the sinner in hell is also to be judged by Him Whose "eyes are as a flame of fire and out of Whose mouth goeth a two-edged sword." The glorious Gospel of free grace in no way cancels the fact of personal accountability to God. He Who makes no exceptions must some day sift our lives.

AUGUST 16

And Hezekiah received the letter of the hand of the messengers, and read it: and Hezekiah went up into the house of the Lord, and spread it before the Lord. And Hezekiah prayed before the Lord (II Kings 19:14, 15).

A message, brief and ominous, has come from Sennacherib. And Scripture gives us a wonderful record (vss. 15-19) of the words of Hezekiah, a great king who knew how to pray. As he bowed before the Lord, Hezekiah did five things. First, he acknowledged the exclusive supremacy of God ("O Lord God of Israel . . . Thou art the God, even Thou alone"). Second, he asked God to take cognizance of what was happening ("Lord, bow down Thine ear, and hear: open, Lord, Thine eyes, and see: and hear the words of Sennacherib"). Third, he recounted the wickedness of Assyria ("Of a truth, Lord, the kings of Assyria have destroyed the nations of their lands"). Fourth, he sought salvation for himself and his people ("Now therefore, O Lord our God, I beseech Thee, save Thou us out of his hand"). Fifth, he asked that *all* nations might know the Lord's supremacy—i. e., the motive of his prayer was the glory of God and the blessing of humanity ("that all kingdoms of the earth may know that Thou art the Lord God").

What a model for prevailing prayer! Is it any wonder that Isaiah sent the king this word of the Lord, "That which thou hast prayed to Me against Sennacherib king of Assyria I have heard"?

AUGUST 17

Let all bitterness, and wrath, and anger, and clamour, and evil speaking, be put away from you, with all malice (Eph. 4:31).

That little word "all," if we really heed it, is a mighty sharp goad to our consciences. The apostolic exhortation, you see, is comprehensive. It does not discriminate between different forms of bitterness, wrath, and the like. Nor does it say that evil speaking is ever permissible. Instead, it plainly says that *all* of these things must be put away from us believers. So let us look into our hearts today and see whether we are cherishing some small bitterness, or just a little anger. See if we have been guilty of harboring a morsel of malice or whether we have indulged in a few sentences of evil-speaking. Then let us recall that all of these things are forbidden, and ask our God through Christ to forgive us and cleanse us from these sins and to help us put them entirely out of our lives.

AUGUST 18

For the fruit of the Light is in all goodness and righteousness and truth (Eph. 5:9).

To be sure, the Authorized Version of this verse speaks of "the fruit of the Spirit," but the best manuscripts have the word "Light" instead of "Spirit." The "Light" referred to is none other than He Who said, "I am the Light of the World" (John 8:12). He is the *phos*, the great Light. And as He indwells believing hearts, He brings forth the threefold fruit of "*all* goodness" (how much that comprehends!), righteousness, and truth. It is through this fruit that the Light shines. "All goodness and righteousness and truth" constitute the filament through which Christ is manifested to the world. We either have the Light or we do not have Him. If we are Christians, we have Him. But what if, having the Light, we lack the threefold filament of all goodness and righteousness and truth? No matter how powerful the current, a lamp is useless without a filament. May we who have the Source of Light indwelling us let Him bring forth His fruit to shine in our lives!

AUGUST 19

He will ever be mindful of His covenant (Ps 111·5)

For our reassurance and comfort today let us italicize one word of this sentence. "He will *ever* be mindful of His covenant." There never can and never will be a time when He will go back on His pledged Word to His people, whether that Word be the Old Testament covenants to the Jews or the New Testament promises to the Church. God will ever, at all times and in all places, remember His Word.

Would you make this text exceeding precious to your heart? Then take your New Testament, find some of your Lord's promises to His own, and bring those promises into God's holy Presence. Say to Him on your knees, "Lord, here are these promises. Thy Word says that Thou wilt ever be mindful of Thy covenant. Therefore, Lord, remember me now for good, according to Thy pledged Word."

AUGUST 20

And thou his son, O Belshazzar, hast not humbled thine heart, though thou knewest all this (Dan. 5:22).

To be teachable is a great virtue. Those who cannot learn either from their own experience or that of others face grave difficulty. This was the fatal flaw in the character of Belshazzar; he was not teachable. Nebuchadnezzar's disaster was nothing to him. Though his predecessor fell through pride, he went on in the same mad course of self-exaltation. This is the charge that the aged prophet brings against the carousing king whose doom is so swift and sure.

Today we have a far richer heritage of experience and inspired counsel than a Belshazzar ever had. And the man or woman who deliberately ignores it, refusing to be taught of God, may have the same charge laid against him: "Thou . . . hast not humbled thine heart, though thou knewest all this." Simply because of what we Christians know and the light God has given us, wilful and proud self-exaltation is a deadly serious matter.

AUGUST 21

For God hath not given us the spirit of fear; but of power, and of love, and of a sound mind (II Tim. 1:7).

When fear comes knocking at the gate of your mind, you may be absolutely certain of its source. Remember that fear is *never* from God. Paul settles that in this inspired word which we take to our hearts today. "God," he says, "hath *not* given us the spirit of fear." And John reinforces him, as he writes in his First Epistle, "God is love . . . there is no fear in love, for perfect love casteth out fear." You may set it down, therefore, as a spiritual axiom, that fear comes only and entirely from the enemy of your soul. And you will find that axiom of immense practical value in overcoming fear. No matter how subtle its guise, recognize its source and you have gone far to defeat it. Then abide in the perfect love of Christ and you will have gone all the way in the overthrow of fear.

AUGUST 22

. . . *but (the spirit) of power, and of love, and of a sound mind* (II Tim. 1:7).

These are the gifts with which our God matches the devil's weapon of fear. Let us look closely at the last of them, "a sound mind." The Greek Testament shows us that this noun (it is one word in the Greek) is derived from the very same verb which describes the Gadarene demoniac, as Luke beautifully pictures him, "sitting at the feet of Jesus, clothed, and in his right mind." Although some of the newer translations render it as "discipline" or "sound judgment," it would seem that this is a case where the Authorized Version is the more accurate. And what a message it brings for our day, when mental and nervous unbalance are so widespread! Along with the spirit of power and of love, God has given His children the spirit of a sound mind. Yes, our God is interested in our nervous and mental as well as physical health. The mind that rests in His truth and believes in His promises is a sound mind.

AUGUST 23

Lead me to the Rock that is higher than I (Ps. 61.2).

There is one unfailing characteristic of the path God chooses for us. Its ultimate direction is ever upward. Like the mountain trail it may dip down into a valley, yet it does not stop there, but goes on higher. When God guides a man through life, He always guides him to upper levels. But mountain climbing is hard work, just because it is an upward pull. And the Christian life is a strenuous life because it is an ascending life. There is a sense in which Bishop Heber's hymnodic reference to the martyrs applies to all of us believers:

"They climbed the steep ascent of Heaven
'Mid peril, toil, and pain."

Yes, let us ask God to lead us to the Rock that is higher than we, but let us remember that we ourselves must climb there.

AUGUST 24

And God wrought special miracles by the hands of Paul (Acts 19:11).

"Special miracles." The meaning appears to be that at this place in his life, Paul had the power of doing miracles that were different from the regular apostolic miracles of healing. What these extraordinary miracles were is clear from the next verse, where it is stated that, when handkerchiefs and aprons belonging to the sick were brought to Paul, cures were effected.

Behind the incident we see how God works in behalf of His servants. At Ephesus Paul was faced with terrific demonic opposition. The Gospel of Christ was challenging the blackness of ancient superstition. There was an extraordinary need, and God gave Paul extraordinary means with which to meet it. So we have a picture of God's faithfulness to His servants. No opposition can be so unusual as to prevent God from supplying the victorious answer to it. When there is a very special need in our life and work for Him, He stands ready to supply us with special help.

AUGUST 25

*Thou wilt keep him in perfect peace, whose mind is stayed
on Thee: because he trusteth in Thee* (Isa. 26:3).

A condition accompanies this promise. According to these
lovely words, perfect peace depends upon a mind that is re-
lying upon God. There is a beautiful undertone of meaning
in the Hebrew words for "stayed" and "trusteth" in this verse.
The first means "sustain" or "support" and the second
"lean on."

After all, is it not true that Christians ought to be serene?
At all times the Christian should have a certain imperturb-
ability of spirit that, while far from insensitive, is yet the
opposite of fretfulness and worry. And the secret of that kind
of serenity lies in its foundation. The mind that is sustained
and supported by God, the heart that really leans on Him,
does have security at all times.

AUGUST 26

He giveth His beloved in sleep (Ps. 127:2, R. V. Margin).

Although the Authorized Version reads, "He giveth His beloved sleep," the preposition "in" may be included in the verse.
What a difference the little word makes. Perhaps the chief
claim of modern psychology to greatness is its discovery of
the subconscious mind. But what psychology discovered only
recently is here recognized by Scripture.

Consider, for instance, how beautifully this precious promise
allows for the subconscious. Science tells us that our minds
are always active; though we lose consciousness in sleep, the
vast reservoir of our unconsciousness is always stirring. Who
can control it? No man, for man cannot control that which
is outside the range of his consciousness. But God is the Lord
not only of our waking but also of our sleeping self. And
as we slumber, He guards us even in our sleep; He Who knew
us when we "were made in secret and curiously wrought in
the lowest parts of the earth" (Ps. 139:15), controls our unconscious minds and gives to us in sleep. What a comfort this
is to those who are inclined to be fearful and worried! If
God gives to His beloved in sleep, we may put down as a certainty that He only and always gives His beloved those things
which are most needful for them.

AUGUST 27

I opened my mouth, and panted: for I longed for Thy com-mandments (Ps. 119:131).

Surely this is akin to the fourth beatitude, "Blessed are they which do hunger and thirst after righteousness: for they shall be filled." How startlingly alive is the Psalmist's language! "I opened my mouth and panted"—that is the very picture of longing. Have you ever really thirsted after God? Has there ever come a time in your life when you have felt that you simply could not go on without a taste of His living Word? If so, you know that such longing after God brings its certain reward. Christ always satisfies the hungering and thirsting soul. And one of the most blessed glimpses of the redeemed in Heaven is found in the unspeakably lovely words of John on Patmos: "They shall hunger no more, neither thirst any more . . . for the Lamb which is in the midst of the throne shall feed them" (Rev. 7: 16, 17).

AUGUST 28

I waited patiently for the Lord; and He inclined unto me, and heard my cry (Ps. 40:1).

This Fortieth Psalm, while Messianic in character, also applies to the individual believer, particularly in its opening verses, wherein redemption is pictured in many of its aspects. The opening verse has a message for us in this hurried age. We are all at one time or another in the place of waiting for God to act. That is inevitable. He Who does all things after the counsel of His own will has His appointed time for everything. Whether we like it or not, there are times when we must wait upon Him. What we need to learn is how to wait. Impatience with God is worse than folly; it tends toward sin. For impatience with God is tantamount to saying that we know better when He should act than He does. Patient waiting, however, is rewarded. David's experience is universally valid for all believers; in His own good time God does incline unto His children and hear their cry. May we who name the Name of Christ trust Him enough to wait patiently for Him.

AUGUST 29

The prayer of faith (James 5:15).

How various are the prayers, not of different persons, but of the same individuals. Some are formal and public, some intimate and private, some are distraught and agonized. Others are discouraged and distressed, while others are long, and still others very brief. The form of expression, the place and the length—these things matter little. But there is one essential ingredient of every true prayer. It is faith. In His grace God has not even decreed the amount of faith a prayer must contain. Indeed, Christ used the tiniest of seeds as the measure of the faith that, through the prayer-lever, can move a mountain (Matt. 17:20). Yet the fact remains that every effectual prayer must be a *prayer of faith* in the Omnipotent God Whose ear is ever open to the cry of His children.

AUGUST 30

For He shall give His angels charge over thee, to keep thee in all thy ways (Ps. 91:11).

This verse and those other words of comforting assurance that continue down through the thirteenth verse of this beloved Psalm are spiritual effects, not causes. The basis of their realization is found in the ninth verse, where we read, "Because thou hast made the Lord, which is my refuge, even the most High, thy habitation." It is plain, therefore, that to make "the Lord even the most High" your "habitation" is the condition for receiving the blessed security described by the Psalmist. We may briefly put the principle thus: the condition for safety in this life is to abide in Christ. To make the Lord your habitation is the same thing to which Christ referred in John 15 when He spoke of abiding in Him. Beware of the superficial thinking that centers the life in self and the world and then, when the storm comes, claims the promises that belong to those who are really making Christ their habitation.

AUGUST 31

The wind bloweth where it listeth, and thou hearest the
sound thereof, but canst not tell whence it cometh, and whither
it goeth: so is every one that is born of the Spirit (John 3:8).

The words of the Lord Jesus are characterized by a finality
that is without parallel. Even His figures of speech are so absolutely precise that nothing more may be said. Take, for
example, this wonderful sentence, illustrative of the new birth.
How could there be a more perfect figure of the new birth
than the wind? Sometimes it blows with cyclonic force, de-
molishing all in its path; sometimes the Spirit of God has
literally to tear a life up by the roots in order to regenerate
that life. Again, the wind may blow with the soft zephyrs of
spring, and so too may the Spirit gently waft some little
child, raised in Christian surroundings, into the Kingdom.

What is the lesson? Just this: as infinitely various as the
wind, so is the Spirit in His work of regeneration. Consequently it follows that it is both wrong and spiritually misleading to set up any particular kind of Christian experience
as essential for everybody. Individuals are all different, and
the Spirit has His own way of working in each life. There is
one Christ and one salvation, but there are many ways in
which the experience of the new birth may come to human
hearts. Beware of anyone who dares insist that your spiritual
experience conform to his own or anyone else's. "The wind
bloweth where it listeth: so is everyone that is born of the
Spirit." You *must* be born again, but let no one disturb you
by legislating just exactly how the Spirit deals with you.

> *Breathe on me, Breath of God,*
> *Fill me with life anew,*
> *That I may love what Thou dost love,*
> *And do what Thou wouldst do.*
>
> *Breathe on me, Breath of God,*
> *Till I am wholly Thine,*
> *Till all this earthly part of me*
> *Glow with Thy fire divine.*

SEPTEMBER 1

When He giveth quietness, who then can make trouble?
(Job 34:29).

God may see fit to have us endure affliction, suffer disappointment upon disappointment, and sorrow upon sorrow. It may be His perfect will for us to be in a whirlpool of trouble, so that we know not which way to turn. But in and through it all He can give an inner peace and instil deep in our hearts a place of quietness that is a sure retreat from the most overwhelming turmoil. And when our God gives us *that* quietness, "who then can make trouble?"

SEPTEMBER 2

And they that had eaten were about four thousand . . .
(Mark 8:9).

It is worthwhile to read over and meditate upon this miracle of our Lord's feeding of the four thousand, if for no other reason than that it has been overshadowed by the preceding miracle of the feeding of the five thousand. You will find it reported with characteristic succinctness by Mark in the first nine verses of this eighth chapter of his Gospel.

What does the feeding of the four thousand teach? Well, among other things it teaches a very comforting lesson. Christ's gracious and supernatural and complete meeting of the needs of His hungry sheep is not an isolated thing. He fed five thousand. A marvelous miracle! But that was not sufficient to satisfy the hunger of the four thousand. And so the Lord Jesus repeated for others, who were weary and in want, the very miracle he had already done.

How true it is of you! You hunger after Him. Yes, there has been that earlier time of blessing, that sacred time of meeting with Him in a wonderful way. But it is past. And past meals do not satisfy today's hunger, nor do past blessings meet needs of the present. Never fear; Jesus Christ is "the same yesterday, and today, and forever." He will come to you all over again in a new and precious way, for He has never disappointed those who trust Him wholly.

SEPTEMBER 3

And He touched her hand, and the fever left her (Matt. 8:15).

The touch of His hand—that was sufficient medicine for the instant healing of Peter's wife's mother. "But," replies some lonely and discouraged Christian, "that was long, long ago. Our Lord is not now here to touch us." Physically that is true, but spiritually and therefore *really* it is false. The Lord Jesus can touch us now. He can lay His hand upon us and still our feverish ways. Truly has Whittier sung:
> "We touch Him in life's throng and press,
> And we are whole again."

You ask how? Through prayer, through meditating upon His Word, through obedient fellowship with Him. In these ways the Lord Jesus draws near to His own with His touch. And it is a transforming touch, changing sorrow into joy, and defeat into victory.

SEPTEMBER 4

Who art thou, O great mountain? before Zerubbabel thou shalt become a plain (Zech. 4:7).

The preceding verse, containing these words, "Not by might, nor by power, but by My Spirit, saith the Lord of hosts," is exceedingly well-known; its sequel, which now speaks to us, is comparatively obscure. But what a message it brings, read and appropriated in its context! It is a glorious invitation to look upon our mountainous difficulties as already leveled. God is speaking, and He is addressing not His servant but His servant's obstacle. He Who works neither by human might nor power, but by the Spirit, challenges the mountain: "Who art thou, O great mountain?" He cries. "Before Zerubbabel thou shalt become a plain."

Christian, God is saying that very thing of your difficulty. For you He says to the mountain, "Before my servant . . ., thou shalt become a plain." Take Him at His Word. Cease to worry; He will level off the obstacle that looms so large right now.

SEPTEMBER 5

*God forbid that I should sin against the Lord in ceasing
to pray for you* (I Sam. 12:23).

Samuel said this after Israel had rejected the theocracy by
demanding a king. Notice the light it sheds upon a certain
form of sin. Samuel was a priest and therefore an intercessor.
And he knew that, as an intercessor, it was his bounden duty
to pray for Israel. Neglect of that duty was nothing less than
sin against the Lord.

Now the believer is a priest. Like Samuel he is an intercessor. And who would deny that what constituted sin for
Samuel constitutes sin for the believer also? Too often we
feel that intercession before God is entirely optional, that we
are under no obligation to exercise the priestly prerogative.
But such is not the case. God expects and requires us to be
faithful in our prayer life. Prayerlessness is sin.

SEPTEMBER 6

The chief priests had delivered Him for envy (Mark 15:10).

There are some ideas common to evangelical Christians that
need re-thinking, and one of them is the idea of what constitutes worldliness. What exactly is meant by separation from
the world? Ask that question of many believers and you will
get a very small answer, a little answer confined to abstaining
from certain practices, such as cards, theatres, smoking, and
drinking. But the world is much bigger than these things.
And many a person who prides himself on being separated
merely because he keeps away from certain amusements and
habits is yet tainted with worldliness. For worldliness is
linked with the sort of sin that ultimately crucified Christ.
Here in our verse for today we have one of its marks—envy.
Think of it! Envy is the sin that led to Christ's crucifixion.
Is it in your heart? Then no amount of abstaining from certain outward things, no matter how necessary that abstention
may be, will make you a truly separated Christian. Let us not
speak about "the separated life" while we are tolerating
in our lives and testimonies such dreadful worldly sins as
pride, gossip, malice, envy, sloth, and impurity.

SEPTEMBER 7

But Ahaz said, I will not ask, neither will I tempt the Lord (Isa. 7:12).

A good deal of downright unbelief is cloaked in false piety. The eleventh verse of this chapter states that God told Ahaz to ask of Him a sign. But Ahaz makes pious objections to God's will. How true the incident is of many of us Christians. God speaks to us about something. We are to offer a rebuke in love, or speak seriously with our brother about his soul. "No," we say, "it would not be courteous to do that. We might be abusing his hospitality." We offer a thousand and one excuses backed by our idea of right. Nevertheless God is speaking. One of the great lessons of the Christian life is to learn to do the will of God, and then to leave consequences to Him.

SEPTEMBER 8

The pride of thine heart hath deceived thee (Obad. vs. 3).

It is a sad fact that one of the deadliest of sins is, in comparison with other sins, not only little feared but sometimes condoned among professing Christians. Consider these two statements, each of them made in reference to an individual church member: (1) "He's a good man, but he's proud." (2) "He's a good man, but he's a thief." The first might pass unchallenged in almost any Christian group; the second immediately stands out as a glaring inconsistency. Yet it is a grave question whether the proud man is not worse in God's sight than the thief. What is the matter? Simply this. Our poor, sin-blinded minds have set up un-Scriptural distinctions between sins. Pride is so prevalent among the religious that we accept it. We need the rude shock of awakening to the fact that the self-righteous proud are guilty of just as damning a sin as theft, murder, or adultery. That is why Christ had to die. "There is none that doeth good, no, not one."

As the Lord looks into your heart today, does He see pride or humility?

SEPTEMBER 9

Through Thy precepts I get understanding: therefore I hate every false way (Ps. 119:104).

Notice the logical sequence. Understanding comes through God's precepts (i.e., through His Word), and understanding issues in hatred of evil. There is much in the world today that passes for true wisdom and understanding, but misses the mark and falls far short of the understanding which is from God. The world has plenty of knowledge, but knowledge alone is devoid of moral force. The understanding which comes from God can always be distinguished by its moral implications; it conduces toward hatred of everything evil. Oh, that we might learn to bring our human wisdom to the test of its relation to evil! Is it making us less sensitive to sin? Is it blunting our hatred of wickedness? Then our wisdom has in it extreme danger to our souls, and should be brought into subjection to the wisdom of God.

SEPTEMBER 10

There is no restraint to the Lord to save by many or by few (I Sam. 14:6).

This word comes from Jonathan as he is about to do one of the most heroic deeds of ancient warfare. Having stated the principle that God's helping of man is not dependent upon circumstances, he acted upon that principle, and overcame with the aid of one armor-bearer the garrison of the Philistines.

The principle he practiced needs to be better known by the Lord's people today. How often we sit back in discouragement with uncompleted work before us. The task is great, and the available means are meager indeed. But we reckon without God, and we forget that "there is no restraint to the Lord to *save by many or by few." Is there just one person standing* with you, just one armor-bearer? Do not hesitate to go out to battle. Are you all alone in the fight? Never fear; Jonathan spoke truth: "There is no restraint to the Lord to save by many or by few."

SEPTEMBER 11

Take ye away the stone (John 11:39).

Did you ever notice the preliminaries to that stupendous miracle of the raising of Lazarus? Among them are these words, "Take ye away the stone." Even Martha, at that command, brought forth the objections of common-sense. But Christ wanted the stone taken away. Surely He Who was shortly to call the dead from the corruption of the grave could have commanded the stone to be removed miraculously, and it would have been removed. But men could move the stone. They could not raise Lazarus.

Is not this God's method? His power *is* available. But there are preliminaries within *our* power that He wants us to accomplish. There are prayer, self-abandonment, earnest faith, and many other acts of stone-moving that lead to God's moving in our behalf.

SEPTEMBER 12

For the wages of sin is death; but the gift of God is eternal life through Jesus Christ our Lord (Rom. 6:23).

"Wages" and "gift." How accurate the Bible is in its nice choice of words! Men and women, boys and girls, work hard for the devil, the master of sin-shackled humanity, for there is in the world no more exacting servitude than that of sin. And the devil is scrupulous in paying off his slaves. At first he rewards them by catering to the flesh and to pride. Later, when the end comes, he pays them their wages in full—death.

But no man may work for eternal life. It is not to be earned, striven for, nor purchased. It is a free gift—the love token of God in the sacrificial shedding of the blood of His beloved Son, the Lord Jesus Christ. Here, then, in these two words, "wages" and "gift," is the great difference between heathenism in all its forms and the pure Gospel of Christ.

Are you working your life away for sin and thus looking forward to your inevitable wages—the death of a Christless eternity? Or have you in your heart received the gift of God, eternal life through faith in the Lord Jesus Christ?

SEPTEMBER 13

Moses wist not that the skin of his face shone (Exod. 34:29).

Perhaps the most beautiful aspect of this radiance of Moses' face was that he was unconscious of it. We may be perfectly certain that Moses did not strive to have a shining face. The glow was not of his own choosing nor the result of his effort; he had been in the Presence of the Most High, and the radiance lingered. Just there is the difference between the modern type of joy, the cultivated smile of an empty heart, and the unconscious light of the indwelling Spirit. Seek the radiance of Christ, not before a mirror, but by beholding Him in His Word and in the secret place of prayer.

SEPTEMBER 14

The whole city came out to meet Jesus (Matt. 8:34).

Here is a verse that begins gloriously and ends tragically. It was after the Lord Jesus had cast out the demons at Gadara. "The whole city came out to meet Jesus." They might have had a revival, they might have received the Son of God. The fame of their belief might have traveled through the ages. But, "when they saw Him, they besought Him that He would depart out of their coasts." Why? Well, the price was too great. He had healed the demon-possessed and had cast the devils into swine. And these people raised swine.

There are many Gadarenes today. They are attracted to Christ, but, when He is unveiled with His message of the Cross that means death to the primacy of material things in human life, the modern Gadarenes beg Him to go. They are glad when the meeting is ended, the appeal for souls finished, the challenge to consecration over. Is there still something of the Gadarene in you? Then beg the Lord not to go, until He has given you strength to deal with that unholy thing.

SEPTEMBER 15

And there was a great calm (Matt. 8:26).

The storm on Galilee pictures a universal bit of Christian experience. When the disciples were in deadly peril and when they realized their danger, they awoke the Lord. In the crisis they turned themselves and their ship over to Him. He spoke, "and there was a great calm."

Have you never been through it, Christian friend? A hopeless situation, blackness before and behind you; you give up, and turn things over to the Captain of your salvation. Then the tumult subsides and He brings His peace to your troubled heart.

But oh, how illogical we are! Instinctively we give our Lord control in our perilous times, but insist on holding the rudder in the smooth seas. Yet all the while there are hidden rocks and treacherous shoals that He only knows. No wonder we meet difficulty and distress of soul. Serenity is a great Christian virtue; and only the surrendered believer, abiding in His Lord, knows what it really is.

SEPTEMBER 16

He shall receive an hundred fold now in this time, houses, and brethren, and sisters, and mothers, and children, and lands, with persecutions; and in the world to come eternal life (Mark 10:30).

"With persecutions." This is the forgotten phrase in Christ's wonderful reply to Peter's rather boastful statement that the disciples had left all to follow Him. Yes, said the Lord, those who have left all for Me shall be paid back a hundred fold what they have left, but this recompense will be accompanied with persecutions.

How natural it is to look only to the promise of reward and forget those two significant words, "with persecutions." They phrase the inescapable lot of every Christian in the world. There is divine reward and blessing, but it is mixed with persecution. If you have made a clean break with sin and the world and if you are standing for the Lord Jesus, there is bound to be persecution. Your Lord has said so, even in the saying in which He promises reward for sacrifice in His Name.

SEPTEMBER 17

For Thou hast been a strength to the poor, a strength to the needy in his distress, a refuge from the storm, a shadow from the heat, when the blast of the terrible one is as a storm against the wall (Isa. 25:4).

What Christian whose experience is in any sense mature can fail to echo this beautiful verse? Our God is all of these things to countless needy souls. And what He has been, that He will continue to be. Man changes, but God abides the same. Perhaps "the blast of the terrible one" will be "as a storm" against the wall of your life. Perhaps hard times of testing are to be your lot. Through it all God will be adequate for your every need, able to do exceeding abundantly above all that you can ask or even think.

SEPTEMBER 18

And when Silas and Timotheus were come from Macedonia, Paul was pressed in the spirit, and testified to the Jews that Jesus was Christ (Acts 18:5).

The marginal reading of the central portion of this passage is quite different from the Authorized Version, and opens up a very profitable line of thought. "Paul," it says, *"was constrained by the Word."* This is a suggestive phrase and, taken with what immediately follows, shows us what happens when a man is immersed in the Word of God. Devotion to the Word must find expression in testimony. Therefore we see in this verse that Paul who gave himself, if any man ever did, to the Word, immediately made use of his increased knowledge in open testimony to the Jews of the Messiahship of Jesus. Surely the record of Paul's life would have been one of vastly inferior service had he refused to act upon the divine constraint induced by the Word. The lesson for us is this: Unless Bible study issues in testimony, its God-given purpose is thwarted. And we know that for any follower of Christ to thwart the purposes of his Lord is a perilous thing.

SEPTEMBER 19

It is time for Thee, Lord, to work . . . (Ps. 119.126).

What a verse for the hour of extremity, when hopes have failed and human plans miscarried! Then is the time for the Lord to work. But in another sense the Lord's time is every time. Perhaps the fact that only in the time of distress do many Christians fall back on Him accounts for much spiritual deadness among believers. To realize that every moment is the Lord's time, to be willing for Him to work *all* the time, in every circumstance of our lives, that is the secret of a happy life in Christ.

SEPTEMBER 20

Will a man rob God? (Mal. 3:8).

Yes, a man will rob God. It is being done every day in all parts of the earth, and it is being done by Christian people, not unbelievers.

Each day every Christian arises with the same precious capital—twenty-four hours that will pass never to return again. Will a man rob God? He will. He will spend all of those hours on himself and on his own, none for God. Or he will spend the great majority of them on his own affairs, giving God only the unused dregs of the day.

Again, God commits to youth physical and mental vigor. Will a man rob God? Look at the tragedy of misspent youth and see the answer.

The years pass. Work is done and money is made. Will a man rob God? The answer is found in the curtailed work of foreign missions and the depleted treasuries of Christian enterprises. God asks all His people, young and old, to give.

And the saddest thing is that all the time God is waiting to *pour* out a blessing upon those who are honestly striving to give Him His just due. "Bring ye all the tithes into the storehouse . . . and prove Me now herewith, saith the Lord of hosts if I will not open you the windows of Heaven, and pour you out a blessing." Let us remember that there are tithes of time and energy as well as tithes of money.

SEPTEMBER 21

I sought him, but I could not find him: I called him, but he gave me no answer (Song of Sol. 5:6).

The experience of the bride with her beloved is the heart-experience of the believer with the Lord. There are times when He withdraws from us. We pray, but He seems far away; we meditate upon the Word, but do not see Him. Often, as we look within ourselves, we see that unconfessed sin is keeping Him away. But there are other times, when we cannot honestly say that deliberate sin is the hindrance. At such times there is but one thing to do, and that is to persevere. Learn to pray through, to retain your hold upon God until He gives the blessing. His testing is for a purpose, and when He once more draws nigh, what joy fills the heart!

SEPTEMBER 22

Fear not: have not I commanded you? be courageous, and be valiant (II Sam. 13:28).

All who are familiar with the glorious first chapter of Joshua will recognize in these words from II Samuel a similarity to that inspiring exhortation (Josh. 1:9). But if they pursue their investigation farther, they will have a shock. For Absalom spoke these words as an incitement to the assassins of his brother, Amnon!

So it is that the devil echoes some of the greatest Bible words. Thus he misuses and misappropriates Scripture. "Fear not . . . be courageous, and be valiant." As if it required real courage to carry through a cowardly assassination! But such are the tactics of the devil. He will stop at nothing, and will even mimic the Word of God to bolster up his dupes in sin.

When something evil comes to us under a religious guise; when sin presents itself decked out in pseudo-scriptural garb; then is the time to beware. The devil is never more dangerous than when quoting the Bible.

SEPTEMBER 23

Why have I grace in thine eyes, that thou shouldst take knowledge of me, seeing I am a stranger? (Ruth 2:10).

This question from the lips of the forlorn Ruth was addressed to Boaz. In one of his poems Keats speaks of Ruth, "when, sick for home, she stood in tears amid the alien corn." And every sinner, lost, homesick, and far from the Father's house, can say to Christ, the Boaz or Kinsman-Redeemer of an estranged world, "Why have I found grace in Thy sight . . . seeing I am a stranger?" Why? There is in us no answer to that question. We have no merit in ourselves. Why? Well, He takes knowledge of us sinful strangers simply because He is love. God loved, and He gave His only-begotten Son.

SEPTEMBER 24

This raised the spirits of all (Acts 27:36, Weymouth).

The scene is Luke's thrilling account of the shipwreck encountered by Paul on his journey as a prisoner to Rome. That the situation was desperate is evidenced by the statement in verse 30, which indicates that the sailors were so stampeded by panic as to attempt to leave the ship with the passengers yet aboard. One of the lasting values of the account of this journey is the picture it gives of Paul's moral grandeur in the time of crisis. Verse 34 shows his practical sense in begging his fellow voyagers to take nourishment. Verse 35 shows his utmost consistency in giving thanks. Any man who, in such a crisis, has time for the public saying of grace, means what he says. It is by no means without reason that, after Paul had done this, the spirits of all were raised.

But why was it that Paul, of all the two hundred seventy-six travellers, stood out as of surpassing courage? The answer is simply that he was the only man aboard who had conquered fear. Having vanquished his own fear, he was in a position to strengthen all who were with him. Thus the price of leadership is always self-control. And the only self-control that can survive a great crisis is that which springs from Christ-control. The root of Paul's moral and physical courage was not in himself but in his Lord.

SEPTEMBER 25

Trust ye in the Lord forever: for in the Lord Jehovah is the Rock of Ages (Isa. 26:4, marginal reading).

It is indeed a treasure that the marginal reading here places at our disposal in substituting "the Rock of Ages" for the far less striking "everlasting strength" of the regular text. "The Lord Jehovah," writes Isaiah, "is the Rock of Ages." But do we know Who that "Lord Jehovah" is? Well, there are many who identify Him with the Lord Jesus of the New Testament, and surely our Lord is worthy of that identification. For He Who was smitten for us in fulfillment of the type of the smitten rock of the wilderness is the very Rock of Ages cleft for the salvation of sinners. Oh, if we would only realize more deeply just Who our Lord is, we should find it easier to trust Him! He Who is the Rock of Ages is a safe foundation for our lives.

SEPTEMBER 26

Look unto Me, and be ye saved, all the ends of the earth (Isa. 45:22).

It is by reason of words like these that the book of Isaiah has been called "the fifth Gospel." Of all the prophetic word it is the most evangelical, being packed with verses that point with inspired clarity to the Saviour. And among these verses our text for today will ever be memorable, because God used it for the conversion of a young Englishman, Charles Haddon Spurgeon, who became the greatest preacher of modern times. It was an uneducated layman, substituting for the absent minister, who was preaching on this text when young Spurgeon came to his church. "Look unto Me, and be ye saved," cried the preacher. And Spurgeon looked and was saved, and, as he said, continued looking all the rest of his life.

Have you ever really looked at Jesus Christ? Have you beheld Him unto your soul's salvation? How simple it all is! Christ does not say, "Serve Me and be saved." He does not demand, "Understand Me and be saved." Nor does He even say in the first instance, "Follow Me and be saved." He only cries out from the depth of His redeeming love, *"Look* unto Me, and be ye saved!"

SEPTEMBER 27

Do ye not therefore err, because ye know not the Scriptures, neither the power of God? (Mark 12:24).

This answer of the Lord Jesus forever reveals the error of all rationalists from ancient Sadducees to present-day unbelievers. Two things are behind that error. And the first is ignorance. The Sadducees, like our own unbelievers, prided themselves on their intellectuality. Whatever the rationalist's vaunted scholarliness, it is usually true that he is ignorant of the Scriptures. The second error of the Sadducees was in the realm of experience—"not knowing the power of God." There is only one way to know God's power and that is through experience gained by trusting Him. To those who have true faith in Him He reveals His mighty power.

Are we safeguarding our lives from the two-fold error of ignorance of Scripture and lack of first-hand, experimental knowledge of God?

SEPTEMBER 28

Commit thy way unto the Lord; trust also in Him; and He shall bring it to pass (Ps. 37:5).

Yes, this is a familiar promise. You may have read it a thousand times, but today it stands before you as new and encouraging as the day you first saw it.

Let us look at it today with some little care. "Commit," it begins. Now the Hebrew word thus translated is *galal*, meaning "roll." So we are reminded that there are times when our way through life becomes a heavy burden. Then it is that we are "to roll" the whole thing—i.e. our entire course through life, including every single care and problem and burden, upon Him Who careth for us.

And what is our Lord's part? Simply this: "And He shall bring it to pass." But take your Bible, beloved, and look carefully at those words. As you do so, you will see that the word "it" is italicized, which means that it is not in the original text. So there is actually in this place a blank. "And He shall bring . . . to pass." O believer, realize that you may fill in that blank with your dearest and most hallowed wish, your deepest need your hardest problem.

SEPTEMBER 29

If he hath wronged thee, or oweth thee ought, put that on mine account; I Paul have written it with mine own hand, I will repay it . . . (Philem. vss. 18, 19).

Here Paul, aged and imprisoned, is "a living epistle" of the Lord Jesus. For, just as he was willing to pay out of his own funds all the money the fugitive slave Onesimus owed Philemon, so Christ will pay all the debt of sin we owe to our Master, God. There is pathos in the half-blind Paul's writing those words with his faltering hand. But there is the power of salvation in the truth that Christ seals our pardon in the blood of His Cross. Do you think Onesimus loved Paul for what he did? Then how much more should you and I, runaway slaves of sin, love our Emancipator and Redeemer, Jesus Christ.

SEPTEMBER 30

Behold, bless ye the Lord, all ye servants of the Lord, which by night stand in the house of the Lord (Ps. 134:1).

Someone once gave a message on this verse entitled, "The Night Life of the Christian." To be sure, the little Psalm in which it occurs was written expressly for the ancient temple worship. Yet it is by no means devoid of meaning for us Gentile believers of a latter day. Much is written, and quite properly so, about the necessity for morning prayer. But night also has its peculiar appropriateness for prayer. One of the most hallowed experiences of the Christian life is to be alone with God when the day's work is done, to stand by night in the presence of the Lord, blessing Him for all the mercies of the day. And there are also those occasional times of communion we may have with Him very late at night. No believer who has experienced sleeplessness and who has committed his sleeplessness to God will ever forget how near the Lord draws in the dead of night. There is no better prescription for insomnia than to turn the wakeful hours into a time of prayer and fellowship with the Lord. Those who do so will find that God still "giveth His beloved sleep."

OCTOBER 1

Everything that is Mine is Thine, and everything Thine is Mine (John 17:10, Weymouth).

This fragment from Christ's great high priestly prayer shows us our Lord both in His likeness to us and in His uniqueness. The first statement is one into which every Christian should be able to enter. He should be able to say to the Father, as did the Lord Jesus, "Everything that is mine is Thine." Have you said that to God out of a life fully given over to Him? . . . But what of the last clause—"Everything Thine is Mine"? Truly that is a stupendous claim which no mere man can ever make. Think of it! Christ is saying with sublime assurance that everything God has is His. That is nothing less than a claim to omnipotence as well as to all the other attributes of Deity. Is it not marvelous that so great a Saviour as Christ came to earth and condescended to share our humanity, even to the extent of being "tempted in all points like as we are yet apart from sin"?

OCTOBER 2

And Amaziah said to the man of God, But what shall we do for the hundred talents which I have given to the army of Israel? And the man of God answered, The Lord is able to give thee much more than this (II Chron. 25:9).

At this point King Amaziah made a noble decision. Organizing an expedition against Edom, he had hired an army of mercenaries from the kingdom of Israel at a cost of close to $2,000,000. But a man of God came and told him that such a linking with Israel, from whom God had departed, was dangerous. On the great assurance of the man of God that "God is able to give much more" than $2,000,000, Amaziah acted. He preferred God to gold.

We Christians face similar decisions. There come times in our lives when human plans must be scrapped, even at financial sacrifice, for God is speaking to us. In our dealings with God it does not pay to be too careful of the dollars. God is able to give us much more than them. To Amaziah He gave victory over the enemy, and He will do as much for us when we really learn to place Him before things.

OCTOBER 3

When I am weak, then am I strong (II Cor. 12:10).

Here is the secret of power in Christian work. And what a grand paradox it is! Only in our weakness can we be really strong for God. Self-reliance appeals to the world, but self-reliance is not one of the great Christian virtues. The path to power for Christ is self-abasement, realization of the individual's nothingness, a sense of utter unworthiness in contrast to the full perfection of the Lord Jesus. Those who cast self aside and depend wholly on Him are the ones who begin to enter into the fellowship of His power.

OCTOBER 4

They are not of the world, even as I am not of the world (John 17:16).

The study of this great prayer reveals the fact that these words are repeated, their first occurrence being at the close of the fourteenth verse. This fact clearly points to their importance; when our Lord says a thing twice, we must make doubly sure to listen. If we think of this sentence as the key to the problem of worldliness, we shall find it invaluable. Christ is telling us believers that we no more belong to the world than He does. It needs to be remembered, moreover, that He spoke these words when He was on earth. His life was lived in constant personal contact with men and women. Nevertheless, in spirit He was separate from the world.

The key to Christ's separation from the world, as well as ours, lies in the preposition "of" (Greek *ek*), which has here the sense of "out of" or "originating from." Christ was separate from the world, because He did not originate out of the world; He came down from above. You and I, while born physically into the world, must be separated from the world spiritually. Through faith in the Lord Jesus we are "born from above" (John 3:3, margin). Let us, therefore, live in accordance with our second rather than our first birth.

OCTOBER 5

But unto every one of us is given grace according to the measure of the gift of Christ (Eph. 4:7).

What a blessing it is that, when it comes to spiritual things, the gift is not given according to our human measure! There are times when we long for more grace, more power, more love, but there are other times when we require these blessings just as urgently but are quite unaware of our need. But God knows. He is not ignorant of our spiritual need. And He supplies it not according to our own estimate, but according to the overflowing "measure of the gift of Christ." Oh, let us be awake to the fact that there never will be a time when Christ will fail to give us of His grace in superabundant measure! The sad thing is that we to whom grace is "given according to the measure of the gift of Christ" so frequently lack the vision to appropriate it all by simple faith.

OCTOBER 6

Things that accompany salvation (Heb. 6:9).

We do well to remember that, although salvation is all that is necessary to insure our entrance into the eternal blessedness of Heaven, it is the beginning of the Christian life. Salvation is the door, and there are other essentials that go with it. One reason for lack of power among many Christians is that they fail to realize the simple fact that there are things that must accompany salvation.

What are these things? Well, we can answer that question very briefly by saying that the Lord would have good works accompany salvation. They have, of course, nothing to do with procuring salvation, but are yet an essential accompaniment and necessary evidence of its reality. Again, praise and worship must go along with salvation. And surely no saved life will grow in spiritual health unless its salvation is followed by testimony.

OCTOBER 7

Brethren, my heart's desire and prayer to God for Israel is, that they might be saved (Rom. 10:1).

This earnest expression of Paul's heart's desire regarding the Jews lays an obligation upon us Gentiles. In writing to the Corinthians Paul says, "Be ye imitators of me, even as I also am of Christ" (I Cor. 11:1). Consequently it behooves us to listen when the apostle speaks personally and urgently, as at the beginning of this tenth chapter of Romans.

Paul's deep longing and fervent prayer were for the salvation of Israel. Do we imitate him in this? How tragic it is to see Christians duped by the vicious anti-Semitism of our day, despising the Jews and bearing them malice. What we need is many more believers who are imitators of Paul in a real heart desire and in true prevailing prayer for Hebrew evangelization. It is extremely doubtful whether any Christian life can be balanced if it is devoid of true concern for Israel.

OCTOBER 8

Jesus which is called Christ (Matt. 27:17).

"Jesus the so-called Christ" is Weymouth's rendering of these words, and it brings out the cynical undertone of Pilate's skepticism. How like the Procurator is much of modern thought. Oh, it would not think of denying the historicity of Christ. It would not question His ethical leadership. But when it comes to His true Deity it turns a dubious eye upon Him. "The so-called Christ." There is a taunt in that phrase which is surely one of the most damning things Pilate ever said. By it he condemned himself even before his condemnation of the Lord Jesus.

What is He to you? Is He "the so-called Christ" and do you have the Pilate view of Him? Is the One Whom the church calls Saviour and Lord really your Christ? Remember that Christ is His Kingly Name. Is He crowned King as well as called King in your life?

OCTOBER 9

Our light affliction . . . (II Cor. 4:17).

The adjective is extraordinary, especially when one considers the life of the man who wrote the phrase. Whatever else he was, Paul was an afflicted man. Plagued by a mysterious thorn in the flesh, his eyesight poor, plotted against, publicly scourged, ship-wrecked, stoned—he knew what afflictions are. Yet here he designated them as "light." Why? Well, read on and you will see that "our light affliction is but for a moment." Paul had before him the ultimate goal. With a true sense of values he knew that, compared with the blessings of eternal fellowship with Christ, any earthly affliction is indeed a light thing. Yes, Christian, the nearer you are to your Lord the lighter will your afflictions become.

OCTOBER 10

Behold the Lamb of God which taketh away the sin of the world (John 1:29).

This wonderful sentence is not only a call to behold Christ; it also describes His work. He is "The Lamb of God, Who *takes away the sin of the world.*" How do you look at sin? Just as the way in which you behold Christ determines your spiritual status, so does the way in which you look at sin. You and I will never appreciate the wonder of our salvation until we realize the sinfulness of sin. "The sin of the world." Think of the sins of past and present—the sins of antiquity and the sins of modern times. Think of the sins of the nations today, and ask yourself whether men have ever been more sinful than now. And that incalculable mountain of sin, which contains your sin and mine, is what "the Lamb of God taketh away." Where does He take it? Well, the 103rd Psalm tells us, "As far as the east is from the west, so far hath He removed our transgressions from us." What has He done to it? Isaiah answers, "Though your sins be as scarlet, they shall be as white as snow; though they be red like crimson, they shall be as wool." How has He done it? By "bearing," as Peter said, "His own self . . . our sins in His own body on the tree." Hallelujah, what a Saviour!

OCTOBER 11

Oh the happiness of the man who hath made Jehovah his trust (Ps. 40:4, Young's Translation).

There are two ways in which you may repeat these words. The first is as the exclamation of an observer. You look about you, you see a thoroughly godly man who is fully trusting the Lord, and you cry out, "Oh, the happiness of the man who hath made Jehovah his trust!" But there is a better way. You look into your own soul, the glory of redemption wells up in your heart, your cup of thanksgiving runs over with the joy of God's faithfulness as you daily trust Him, and you exclaim out of your own experience, "Oh, the happiness of the man who hath made Jehovah his trust!"

Which reading is yours? Are you an observer or an experiencer of this happiness? The answer lies in one simple thing—your own willingness to trust the Lord.

OCTOBER 12

He that believeth on the Son hath everlasting life: and he that believeth not the Son shall not see life; but the wrath of God abideth on him (John 3:36).

The issue could not be more clearly drawn than in this verse. Believe on the Son of God and you have everlasting life here and now. Reject Him and you will not only not see life, but, if you keep on rejecting Him until your death, the wrath of God will abide upon your soul. Nothing could be more solemnly plain. But how many of us are preaching the whole truth of that verse? Oh yes, we say, we witness to Christ. We tell the unsaved of His life and death and resurrection. We tell them of what He has done for us. But, honestly now, how often do we tell them the whole story? John did; he warned of the wrath to come. Paul did; he wrote of the coming judgment. The Lord Jesus did; He spoke of the place where "their worm dieth not and their fire is not quenched." Should we do any less? Or can it be that we know more about what ought to be preached than the Lord and His inspired apostles? We Christians ought to think seriously of the missing note in our modern witness, the note of warning to sinners to flee from the wrath to come.

OCTOBER 13

The dead praise not God (Ps 115:17).

Let us apply this word to the devotional life. Most Christians have experienced times of spiritual deadness. Prayer is difficult. Testimony is hard. Worship is wearying. Yet all the time the soul is longing for God. There is a reason for it all. In many such cases there has been a neglect of praise in the prayer life. "The dead praise not God." Just let your prayers become all petition, just seek from God all the time instead of praising Him, and your spiritual life will dry up. The efficacious prescription for spiritual deadness is to praise God. Praise Him in prayer, in your reading of the Word, in your testimony, and in your work, and there will be a resurrection in your heart.

OCTOBER 14

As soon as they were come to land, they saw a fire of coals there, and fish laid thereon, and bread. Jesus saith unto them, Bring of the fish which ye have now caught . . . Jesus saith unto them, Come and dine (John 21: 9-12).

A blessed truth is contained in these verses. We may put it this way: the Lord Jesus prepares sustenance for those who do His will. Looking back in the narrative, we recall that He told the disciples to cast their net on the right side of the ship, and that they obeyed with the result that they caught an abundance of fish. And then, when they reached the shore with their catch, they found breakfast already prepared by His own hands. The fire was laid; the fish were broiling. He Who had multiplied the loaves and fish to feed the five thousand was Himself preparing to assuage the hunger of His tired disciples. They had obeyed His voice, success was theirs, but He needed not their fish to feed them. Before they ever reached the shore their sustenance had been provided by Jesus. And so He said, "Come and dine." Even so today He invites His obedient servants to receive spiritual sustenance from His own hand. But to receive that sustenance we must come to Him in prayer, in study of the Word, and, when the opportunity is ours, in the communion of His Supper.

OCTOBER 15

God resisteth the proud, but giveth grace unto the humble (James 4:6).

Could there be a plainer demonstration of the sinful folly of pride than these four words, "God resisteth the proud"? Think of it, Christian. When you and I fall into pride—and this includes pride in our spiritual attainments as well as other forms of pride—we have done nothing less than array ourselves against Almighty God. We have shut ourselves out from His grace. God cannot violate His nature; He is the Sovereign of the universe, and He is bound to oppose the folly of pride. Today, earnestly and submissively, let us ask God to make us humble.

OCTOBER 16

When therefore He was risen from the dead, His disciples remembered that He had said this unto them; and they believed the Scripture, and the word which Jesus had said (John 2:22).

The Lord Jesus had just spoken of His death and resurrection under the figure of the Temple, but it was not until after these events happened that His disciples really understood His word. John's inspired comment on this matter is very enlightening. The disciples, he says, "believed the Scripture, and the word which Jesus had said." Even brief meditation is sufficient to show us the indissoluble union between the word of our Lord and Scripture. When the disciples believed Scripture, they believed the Lord.

So it is with men today. If only they would realize that it is never a light thing to disbelieve Scripture, for the plain reason that disbelief of Scripture is nothing less than disbelief of the Lord Himself! While John's comment has its primary application to a single event in the early life of the Lord Jesus, its underlying meaning extends to all the Bible from beginning to end. Just as it is not a light thing to disbelieve Scripture, so it is never a matter of small moment to believe it. When a man believes the Bible, he believes God; and when he believes God, God Himself in faithfulness to His Word is on his side.

OCTOBER 17

The Lord raiseth them that are bowed down (Ps. 146:8).

There are two ways of being bowed down—either by force
of external circumstances, or through dejection of one's own
spirit. In either case it takes someone outside of self to lift
one up. No one of any maturity who reads these words has
escaped periods of being bowed down through one cause or
another. Nor will anyone reading them escape the experience
of being bowed down in the future. Doubtless there are those
who are fearfully burdened this very day. Let such know
assuredly that the Lord Who "raiseth up those that be bowed
down" is none other than He Who said, "Come unto Me, all
ye that labor and are heavy laden, and I will give you rest."
And if we are walking erect and joyful today, let us praise
God for having raised us to the posture of victory.

OCTOBER 18

The sword of the Spirit, which is the Word of God (Eph.
6:17).

John Bunyan was right in picturing the struggle between
Christian and Apollyon as centered round the sword of the
Spirit. For that sword is our one offensive weapon. Unless
we know how to use it, we are noncombatants in the spiritual
warfare. The armour of God will protect us, but without the
sword of the Spirit we can strike no blow for Christ. Like
civilians in a besieged fort we are mere observers of the
battle.

But let us who would rout the enemy remember a very
simple thing. We cannot wield a sword that we do not possess.
Said the Psalmist, "Thy Word have I hid in my heart . . ."
Unless, therefore, the Word of God is in our hearts and minds
and upon our tongues we cannot wield it skillfully in the
battle "against principalities, against powers, against the
rulers of the darkness of this world, against spiritual wickedness in high places." Yes, believers, you must learn to know
the Word of God well enough to use it as your spiritual sword,
or else you are a shirker in the cause of Christ.

OCTOBER 19

Let me pull out the mote out of thine eye (Matt. 7:4).

There may be times when a Christian is called upon to perform that duty. But such times are much more rare than many think. And when they do come, they require a sanctified sensitiveness that only the Holy Spirit can give. Mote pulling is a delicate business. The eye, as some one has suggested, is not to be operated upon with a buzz saw and washed out with boiling water. And the soul is even more tender. Yet how carelessly we sometimes treat it with the abrasive of unloving tactlessness and the caustic of a biting tongue!

OCTOBER 20

Even so, come, Lord Jesus (Rev. 22:20).

It is doubtless true that not for many a year have so many Christians been praying these words of the beloved disciple as today. Today, when ruthless warfare is being waged, when we see the collapse of cherished hopes for a peaceful world, when our prayers for peace are not answered here and now, there remains yet this great cry of invitation. It came in the first instance out of suffering, as it was penned by the exiled disciple in Patmos. He had seen the heavens opened; the future ages had been unrolled before his rapt gaze; he had seen the rise of unspeakable wickedness upon earth, the final defiant gesture of evil, and the coming of the Lord in power and great glory. And his final cry was, "Even so, come, Lord Jesus." That cry is not only an invitation. It is also a confession. It means that men have failed. Without Christ they cannot administer justice and cope with monstrous iniquity. Have we not learned at last that peace without Christ is delusive? Then let us pray. O Christian, let us pray for the soon intervention of the Lord Jesus Who *is* coming again and Whose right it is, and His alone, to rule this suffering world.

OCTOBER 21

The common salvation (Jude, vs 3)

Jude's adjective in this phrase is worthy of note. It means just what it says, that salvation is a *common* thing in the sense that it is not the private possession of any special class or group. When it comes to the mercies of God, there is no aristocracy; Christ died for the whole world, and God would have all men to be saved. That being the case, what a despicable thing it is for those who have received the common salvation to keep it just for themselves alone. Jude's phrase is in itself a powerful argument for missions. If salvation is what he says it is—common and for all—then it simply must be made known to the whole world.

OCTOBER 22

I gave my brother Hanani . . . charge over Jerusalem: for he was a faithful man, and feared God above many (Neh. 7:2).

An interesting study in the true values of life would be to list all the terms of commendation given individual men and women in the Bible. From Enoch down through Demetrius one would find certain significant qualities held up for approval. Here is an example; Hanani is praised for faithfulness and for fearing God—characteristics that must belong to every Christian. How different is God's scale of value from that of men. Men commend talent, wealth, power, fame, yet one might search Scripture from cover to cover without finding a man praised for mere possession of wealth, for instance. This being true, it is a grave question whether any Christian is justified in giving his life to the pursuit of those things that God considers unworthy of praise. One of the most difficult choices a child of God makes is the choice between the good and the better, the merely permissible and the essential.

OCTOBER 23

Now on whom dost thou trust, that thou rebellest against me? (II Kings 18:20).

Rab-shakeh is acting as Sennacherib's spokesman. And this question gives us insight into the battle with evil which we, no less than Hezekiah, must fight. "That thou rebellest against me." Let Sennacherib represent Satan, the besieger of every Christian heart, and we begin to see the abiding lesson of these words. Just as Hezekiah rebelled against the Assyrian oppressor, we must rebel against the dark oppressor of our souls. No one can remain truly Christian and maintain a passive relation to Satan. In respect to evil we must all be rebels. Even though the devil may gain temporary control over some portion of our lives, we must rebel, trusting in the same Lord Who conquered the devil in the wilderness. The degree to which we are revolting against Satan and all his subordinate forces is the measure of our usefulness for Christ.

OCTOBER 24

Moreover I will endeavour that ye may be able after my decease to have these things always in remembrance (II Peter 1:15).

The exhortation to remember is one of the key-notes of this first chapter of Peter's last letter. As the chapter draws to a close, the apostle brings forth two things to authenticate his teaching regarding the Christian character and life. The first, referred to in verses 16-19, is the transfiguration of Christ. The second is set forth in verses 19-21, and is the Scriptures, particularly in their prophetic aspect. Peter's mention of the transfiguration focuses attention upon an outstanding experience of Christ, which God gave him; his reference to the prophetic Word centers in the Bible.

The lesson in this is that of the necessary balance between experience and the Word. Experience alone, even such a transcendent experience as Peter had at the transfiguration, may be dangerous unless balanced by the Word. On the other hand, the Word alone may become cold and intellectual unless warmed by experience. Each is essential and each complements the other. Experience must ever be backed by the Word; the Word must always be vitalized by experience.

OCTOBER 25

My God shall supply all your need according to His riches in glory by Christ Jesus (Phil. 4:19).

When God gives His children a promise like this, He expects them to believe it implicitly. But there is a difference between belief and presumption in this matter of trusting the promises of our loving heavenly Father. It is therefore essential for us to note exactly what God promises and to trust Him to do what He promises and that only. We have no right, for instance, on the basis of our verse for today to ask God for certain things that we think we need and then blame Him for not giving them to us. Behind every one of our petitions there must be the acknowledgment that He and He alone knows what our needs really are. Keeping this in mind will prevent much discouragement over "unanswered" prayer. God will indeed supply every need of His children, but only He in His infinite and loving wisdom is the final judge of what we need.

OCTOBER 26

For this shall every one that is godly pray unto Thee in a time when Thou mayest be found: surely in the floods of great waters they shall not come nigh unto Him (Ps. 32:6).

Let us take comfort today in two phrases occurring in this verse. They are these: "in a time when Thou mayest be found" and "in the floods of great waters." David is talking about the prayers of those whose transgressions are forgiven and sins covered. After full confession has been made unto God, they come to God and find that their time of distress, yes, even "in the floods of great waters," is the very time when He may be found.

Oh, does this not show us that perilous days carry with them their peculiar assurance of God's nearness? The floods of calamity may sweep the world, but they shall not come nigh the soul of the godly. In the great waters of today He Who came walking over troubled Galilee to comfort His frightened disciples is found ready to help His own.

OCTOBER 27

The Lord seeth not as man seeth; for man looketh on the outward appearance, but the Lord looketh on the heart (I Sam. 16:7).

This divine word is a source of great comfort for the children of God. How often the world misunderstands our motives. Yes, how often even fellow Christians misunderstand and misrepresent us. But God knows. He sees beneath the surface. He knows the very intent of our hearts. And because He knows He understands. It makes it easy to bear the reproach of men when we are sure that our Lord knows all. As a familiar hymn puts it, "Jesus knows our every weakness."

OCTOBER 28

For I was ashamed to require of the king a band of soldiers and horsemen to help us against the enemy in the way . . . So we fasted and besought our God for this: and He was intreated of us (Ezra 8: 22, 23).

Ezra had a great responsibility. He was not only leading back to Jerusalem a large company of exiles, but he also had in his charge a sacred treasure of gold and silver vessels. His reason for not asking the king for an armed escort is found in the latter half of verse 22 of this chapter—"because we had spoken unto the king, saying, The hand of our God is upon all them for good that seek Him; but His power and His wrath is against all them that forsake Him." So Ezra chose to trust God rather than a military guard, with the result that he arrived safely in Jerusalem with the returning exiles unmolested and the sacred treasure intact.

This historical event is a parable of Christian living. There come times when we must choose between human security and God's promises. Happy are those who, in abandonment to God, refuse the help of the world. They are the ones who will arrive at the New Jerusalem not alone, but accompanied by a band of many turned to righteousness. They will present their treasure intact before the Lord of lords and King of kings.

OCTOBER 29

The Name of the Lord is a strong tower: the righteous runneth into it, and is safe (Prov. 18:10).

Extended comment on this glorious verse is superfluous; with unmistakable directness it speaks its message of assurance. But pause just a moment to note who "the righteous" are. Obviously this expression means believers, for only those clad with the imputed perfection of Christ are righteous in the sight of our Holy God. Therefore, if you are a believer, this verse applies to you. In the stress of life today you can flee to the mighty fortress of Christ's precious Name and find a safe refuge.

OCTOBER 30

And many of the Samaritans of that city believed on Him for the saying of the woman, which testified, He told me all that ever I did (John 4:39).

The woman whom Christ met at the well of Samaria no sooner recognized Him as her Messiah than she became an evangelist, and a very effective one at that. But let us notice especially the substance of her testimony, as recorded in our verse for today. Now there are many good people who would criticize that testimony. They would say that it was incomplete and fragmentary, lacking in a doctrinal basis. Nevertheless the fact remains that God used it mightily. For it had the essential merit of being based upon a true experience of Christ. The woman's testimony was brief, because as yet she knew only a little about her Lord. But what she did know was living for her; it belonged to her first-hand knowledge. And God wonderfully used her words. Thus it is that He graciously blesses the faltering testimony of a simple believer, who knows personally whereof he speaks, more than the theologically correct discourse of one who is preaching things not real to his own heart. There is danger in preaching and witnessing beyond our experience. It is the note of reality that lends power to our testimony for Christ.

OCTOBER 31

*Not by works of righteousness which we have done, but ac-
cording to His mercy He saved us, by the washing of regeneration and renewing of the Holy Ghost* (Titus 3:5).

Packed into this sentence is the whole evangel. "Not by
works of righteousness which we have done." How the world
needs to be taught that foundation truth, so contrary to the
natural impulses and desires of man! Not a single thing we
can do, however good and great, can ever suffice to save us.
The only way any man ever can or will come to Christ is in
the attitude of the great hymn that reflects the words before
us:

> "Nothing in my hand I bring,
> Simply to Thy cross I cling."

That salvation is all of Christ and not in any way of man
is further shown by the rest of the verse: "but according to
His mercy He saved us, by the washing of regeneration and
the renewing of the Holy Ghost." Now regeneration is another
word for rebirth. And just as physical birth is a matter of
forces and powers outside the babe, so our rebirth is entirely
of God and not of self. Thus it is only through the operation
of the Holy Spirit that we are renewed in Christ. Wherefore,
Paul elsewhere cries, "If any man be in Christ, he is a new
creature, old things are passed away; behold, all things are
become new" (II Cor. 5:17).

You say that you know these things and that they are merely
"the Old, Old Story"? But remember that just to the extent
that you are holding on to self-righteousness are you hindering
Christ from bringing to you His *full* salvation.

> *Not the labor of my hands
> Can fulfill Thy law's demands;
> Could my zeal no respite know,
> Could my tears forever flow,
> All for sin could not atone;
> Thou must save, and Thou alone.*

NOVEMBER 1

Be still, and know that I am God (Ps. 46:10).

Another translation reads as follows, "Let be, and know that I am God." "Let be"—surely this implies the giving up of our feverish strivings. There come times in our lives when we just cannot do another thing. We have tried our best. We have struggled and striven and fretted until, as the saying goes, we are "at the end of the rope." Then is the time to "be still," to "let be" and rest in the consciousness of the Godhood, if we may use the term, of God. Simply ceasing from our unavailing efforts and realizing God brings inexpressible comfort because it restores our sense of proportion. For, as we know that God is God, that He is upon the Throne, the things of earth recede to their proper place.

NOVEMBER 2

And there appeared an angel unto Him from Heaven, strengthening Him (Luke 22:43).

Let us tread softly as we meditate upon this sentence, for the place whereon we stand is holy ground. We are in the Garden of Gethsemane. Our Lord sees before Him the cross whereon His thorn-covered head is to be bowed under all the sin of the world. Out of the depths of His inscrutable suffering He prays that perfect prayer, "Father, if Thou be willing, remove this cup from Me: nevertheless not My will but Thine be done." And then we have this precious sentence, peculiar to Luke's Gospel.

Oh, Christian friend, take courage from this holy scene. Although it was the Father's will for Christ to taste that bitter cup, the Father gave His suffering Son supernatural strength for His greatest ordeal. And we too have our times of bitter struggle. Like Paul we cry to God for the thorn to depart. And when it does not depart, we shall always find His Grace sufficient for the need. The Father Who sent the angels to strengthen His Son in Gethsemane will never give us any burden He will not help us bear.

NOVEMBER 3

Troubled on every side, yet not distressed; perplexed, but not in despair; persecuted, but not forsaken (II Cor. 4: 8, 9).

Never be surprised when all these come into your life—trouble, perplexity, persecution, and even dejection. Paul faced them, and they are common to the experience of all Christians who are fighting the good fight. But when they come, be diligent to learn the comforting distinctions which Paul makes in this remarkable series of contrasts. Rest yourself in the assurance that, though your Lord may permit you to have trouble, He would shield you from the distress of worry. Know that, though He may allow you to be sore perplexed, He would not have you despair. Be certain that He Who never, never forsakes the persecuted, will in no wise let His child be cast down to the extent of destruction.

NOVEMBER 4

Occupy till I come (Luke 19:13).

In His parable of the ten pounds Christ puts these words into the mouth of the departing nobleman. But the nobleman being Christ and we the servants, the saying is really from the Lord Himself. Now we do wrong to interpret too narrowly this matter of occupying for Christ. Our Lord means the pounds to be symbols of all of our resources.

With that in mind consider your spiritual resources. If you have any doubt as to what they are, read the first three chapters of Ephesians, and you will see something of the spiritual blessings wherewith God has blessed us in heavenly places in Christ. But what use are we making of the unsearchable riches of Christ? To read about them is interesting, but it is not enough. We must "possess our possessions" in the Lord. He would have us actually occupy His Word until He come.

O Christian, what are you doing with the glorious promises of God's Holy Word? Are you merely admiring them, or are you occupying them through the faith that looks to God to do all that He has promised?

NOVEMBER 5

And He hath put a new song in my mouth, even praise unto our God: many shall see it, and fear, and shall trust in the Lord (Ps. 40:3).

This is a wonderful thing that God does for us Christians. Having lifted us out of the horrible pit and miry clay, having set our feet upon the rock, He daily establishes our steps. And as we walk in the safety of His leading, He gives us a song to sing. That song is "Praise unto our God," as David tells us in this Fortieth Psalm. And it has a far wider function than the mere edification of the singer. For "many shall see it, and fear, and shall trust in the Lord." The song of praise is therefore a testimony that God uses for the salvation of many.

God Himself puts that song in our mouths. But He does not sing it for us. We must do that. And until we sing the song of the redeemed our testimony is incomplete. If we are longing for the salvation of many, let us be very sure that our witness does not leave out the song of "Praise unto our God."

NOVEMBER 6

Neither do I condemn thee: go and sin no more (John 8:11).

And so our Lord dismissed the woman who in all her shame had been brought before Him. Without condemnation He sent her away in the freedom of His forgiveness. "Go," He said. But He did not stop there, for He added these four words—"and sin no more." Yes, He sent the woman away uncondemned, graciously forgiven, but He sent her away with the solemn understanding that she was to sin no more.

This is the principle on which our Lord is always dealing with sinners. Whatever be our transgression, He will forgive. But the purpose of His forgiveness is that we might sin no more. To receive acquittal from the Son of God, to hear His pardoning "Go," purchased with His own blood, and then to go out and sin the same sin all over again—that is to pervert the purpose of His grace. Forgiveness is free, but never to the extent of countenancing the repetition of sin.

NOVEMBER 7

The Lord knoweth how to deliver the godly out of temptations (II Peter 2:9).

Are you tried to the breaking point? Are things too much for you, problems seemingly insoluble, burdens too great to be borne, the arrows of the devil numerous and wounding? Then here is comfort from impetuous Peter who knew more than most of the apostles what temptation meant. No, you cannot see your way out. But *God can.* God knows just how to deliver the godly (His own through faith in Christ) out of temptation.

NOVEMBER 8

Manasseh . . . reigned fifty and five years in Jerusalem . . . and he did that which was evil in the sight of the Lord (II Kings 21: 1, 2).

See how the record of this wicked king's reign continues: "He built up again the high places . . . he reared up altars for Baal . . . and worshipped all the host of heaven . . . and he made his sons pass through the fire . . . and dealt with wizards" (vss. 3-6). But there is not time to list all the evil that Manasseh did. Every reform his father had instituted he set out systematically to nullify.

Why was Manasseh allowed to break down the good his father had done? The answer is hidden deep in God's permissive will. But, though we cannot explain it, we can see a law of the moral economy behind this shocking reign. Evil loses no time in trying to undo good. This lost world is so constituted that good, if left to itself, lacks permanency. Like the garden it must be cultivated or else the weeds of sin will choke the flowers of virtue. The great failure of most reforms is that they are not kept up.

So also with the individual life. The garden of your soul must be tended carefully if you are not to slip back into a Manasseh time of apostasy. Happy is the Christian who keeps his life in good repair through constant submission to the indwelling Spirit of Christ.

NOVEMBER 9

And I will very gladly be spent for your souls (marginal reading, II Cor. 12:15).

Here the great apostle voices one of the most noble motives of Christian service—a love for souls. You and I have the precious gift of life. And one thing is certain; as the years pass we must spend our lives. Whether we will or not, time goes on and life is used up. The only question, then, is in what cause, to what purpose, shall we be spent? Christian, can you resist the call to be spent in the service of Christ for the souls of others?

NOVEMBER 10

The impotent man answered Him, Sir, I have no man, when the water is troubled, to put me into the pool: but while I am coming, another steppeth down before me. Jesus saith unto him, Rise, take up thy bed, and walk (John 5: 7, 8).

The impotent man learned one of the greatest lessons we believers need to learn. He learned that Christ can do the impossible. For thirty-eight hopeless years the impotent man had gazed longingly at the healing waters of Bethesda. But when it came to his stepping down into them, there might as well have been a mountain in the way. Yet what was an insurmountable obstacle to the impotent man was nothing to Christ. He needed no intermediate aid of troubled waters to give strength to the weak. His word was pure omnipotence, and with His word He healed the helpless.

Says a writer on the philosophy of education, "To believe all things are possible with either God or man is a vast strain on the credulity of all but the feeblest intellects." Nevertheless, let us Christians dare to believe in the omnipotence of our Saviour and be classed by modern philosophy with "the feeblest intellects" rather than win the favor of the earthly wise by denying the power of our Lord. For we know that, when obstacles loom most mountainous and we are utterly impotent, then it is that Christ shows His omnipotence in our behalf. To those whom philosophy leaves weak and defeated, He only brings the word of life, "Rise, take up your daily task; walk and work for Me."

NOVEMBER 11

I will give thee the treasures of darkness (Isaiah 45:3).

In the divine charge to Cyrus, who was supernaturally named long before his birth, there is this suggestive phrase—"the treasures of darkness." Long, long before Shakespeare wrote "sweet are the uses of adversity," the inspired prophet spoke of "the treasures of darkness." And through the centuries God has been revealing them for the enrichment of His suffering, sorrowing, and persecuted children. Every Christian bed of pain, every Christian house of mourning, every martyr's cell is a place of potential riches of a vastness far beyond the comprehension of those whose lives are only easy and pleasant. "The treasures of darkness." God grant that we may have eyes to see them when we go through our testing times.

NOVEMBER 12

While I was with them in the world, I kept them in Thy Name: those that Thou gavest Me I have kept (John 17:12).

These precious words from our Lord's great prayer of intercession contain shades of meaning not apparent on the surface. For instance, our Greek Testament shows us that there are in this sentence two different words translated "kept." The first word is *tereo*, which is the familiar New Testament term for "keep." But the second word is *phulasso*, which is linked to the word for "prisoner," and therefore means to guard someone as closely as a prisoner is guarded.

What comfort should come to harassed Christians from this double assurance of their blessed Lord's keeping power! He spoke these words definitely of His disciples. Yet we know from the Book of Hebrews that "Jesus Christ is the same yesterday, and today, and forever." He Who both kept and guarded, even as His redeemed prisoners, the disciples, will do exactly the same for us. It must have been a very wonderful thing to have been one of those who lived side by side with the Lord Jesus, but have you ever thought that those early disciples were no closer spiritually to the Lord than you and I may be? We too may trust Him just as they did. We may rely upon Him to keep us just as securely as He kept Peter, James, John and the others of the twelve.

NOVEMBER 13

And having on the breastplate of righteousness (Eph. 6:14).

The breastplate is a most vital piece of armour because it protects the heart. Long ago Solomon said, "Keep thy heart with all diligence, for out of it are the issues of life." And the best protection for the Christian's heart, which the enemy is so constantly assailing, is the breastplate of righteousness. Now this "breastplate of righteousness" has a two-fold meaning. It refers to that perfect righteousness of Christ which is imputed to us when we are born again through faith in the Lord Jesus. And it also means the purity and goodness of character resulting from the Holy Spirit's work in our hearts. Thus we see that the pure heart cleansed by the blood of Christ, and sanctified by the Holy Spirit is the protected heart. Righteousness is the only breastplate that can withstand the assaults which the forces of unrighteousness are making against our very hearts.

NOVEMBER 14

But when the morning was now come, Jesus stood on the shore: but the disciples knew not that it was Jesus (John 21:4).

This final chapter of the Gospel of John is full of lessons for work. It begins with a group of the disciples fishing unsuccessfully during the night. Morning comes and they see Jesus standing on the shore. Surely the inference is permissible that He had been there for some time, perhaps watching their work the whole night through. And when the dawn came He stood waiting for them, although the disciples did not immediately recognize Him. Nevertheless, unrecognized though He was, the Lord Jesus was there.

Let us learn from this detail of an incident that happened so long ago the abiding truth that Jesus always stands by His toiling servants. They may be laboring in the night, wrapped in the darkness of obscurity, far from the plaudits of men. Yet their Lord is always waiting nearby, ready to help, and when the veil is lifted His servants see Jesus at hand. Yes, we may set it down as a spiritual principle and comforting fact that where Christians are working, Christ is watching.

NOVEMBER 15

My thoughts are not your thoughts (Isaiah 55:8).

We need search no farther than this for the reason why it is an absolute necessity for us Christians to lay up God's Word in our hearts. Our thoughts are not God's thoughts. Between the mind of the Almighty and that of the sinner there is a great gulf. The only way for us to do God's will is to know and think His thoughts; and the only way to think His thoughts is to hide His Word in our hearts. When we Christians read our Bibles, we are not just acquainting ourselves with great inspirational literature; we are doing a thing that, along with prayer, is absolutely essential for the health of our souls and the practice of our faith.

NOVEMBER 16

If a soul shall sin through ignorance against any of the commandments of the Lord . . . then let him bring for his sin . . . a young bullock without blemish unto the Lord for a sin-offering (Lev. 4:2, 3).

It is instructive to note in the opening chapters of Leviticus that the first three offerings — the burnt, meal, and peace-offerings—were voluntary, but that the sin and trespass-offerings were compulsory. The order of their mention is not the order of actual practice, the burnt-offering being set forth first because it points to the full perfection of Christ. But in man's personal approach to God there was no choice; the sin-offering *had* to come first.

Nearly two thousand years ago the sacrificial ritual ceased. Nevertheless, the spiritual principles it illustrated are changeless, and chief among them is the fact that the man who would approach God must first have his sin dealt with. Though modern religion loves to talk about various "approaches" to God, there is only one way for anyone to draw nigh to Him, and that is by way of the Cross upon which Christ, the Lamb of God, was slain for the sin of the world.

NOVEMBER 17

The Light shines in the darkness, and the darkness has never overpowered it (John 1:5, Weymouth).

The world lies in the evil one. It is darkened by reason of sin. Yet black as sin is, it cannot extinguish the True Light. He shines on, and no sin is so dark as to overpower the healing rays that shine from His Cross. We Christians need to remind ourselves that the Lord Jesus really *is* the Light of the world. We need to remember that He is the Victor and that no evil can stand before His searching gaze. "His eyes," wrote John in his Patmos vision, "were as a flame of fire . . . and His countenance as the sun shineth in his strength."

NOVEMBER 18

If ye then be risen with Christ, seek those things which are above, where Christ sitteth on the right hand of God (Col. 3:1).

Thus begins one of the noblest exhortations in all Scripture. Paul implies that experience of a new life in Christ, glorious though it is, is not enough. Life must always have a goal. And for those who have become new creatures in Christ Jesus anything less than the highest goal is unthinkable.

"Seek those things which are above, where Christ sitteth on the right hand of God." Think about that injunction, and you will see how much it rules out. Why, it rules out *everything* that is of this world. What Paul is saying by implication is this: the things of the world can never be the goal of a consecrated Christian life. Not even the finest of human endeavors are good enough to be sought with the whole heart by those whom Christ has raised together with Him. To be sure, we must give our attention to certain things of this world. Some of them, such as literature and art and science, may be very beneficial in their places. But they can never be the object of our soul's deepest desire.

In the light of this truth, ask yourself upon what your heart is set. What actually are you most ardently seeking in life— a deeper, fuller knowledge of your Lord and all the beauties of His grace, or something that is only of this world?

NOVEMBER 19

Then Isaac sowed in that land, and received in the same year an hundredfold: and the Lord blessed him (Genesis 26:12).

Look up the context of this verse and you will see that it follows the account of Isaac's deplorable sin at Gerar. Like Abraham, his father, he told a cowardly lie about his wife. But God did not cast him off. He knew the heart of Isaac and knew that the desire of Isaac was really toward Him. Verily our God is a God of unbounded mercy! And what about Isaac? Well, he "sowed in that land." In other words, unlike some Christians who have fallen, he did not cease working. The blessing came to him, but he had first to sow. Is your fellowship ever broken with God? Confess your sin, go to Christ for cleansing and then—work.

NOVEMBER 20

Have not I commanded thee? Be strong and of a good courage; be not afraid, neither be thou dismayed: for the Lord thy God is with thee whithersoever thou goest (Josh. 1:9).

There are few more striking portions of the Word of God than the first nine verses of Joshua. Moses had died, and the heavy responsibility for leading a whole nation into the Promised Land had fallen upon Joshua. How gloriously Joshua discharged his commands is set forth in the book bearing his name. And surely the secret of his success is found in our verse for today.

"Have not *I*," saith the Lord, "commanded *thee?*" It makes, you see, all the difference in the world as to who issues a command. In this case it was the Lord Himself Who ordered Joshua to be strong and courageous, and it was the same Lord Who promised to be his constant companion. Let us believers of a latter day be perfectly certain that the same Lord Who commanded Joshua also commands us. He orders us to be strong and of a good courage. He tells us to be neither afraid nor dismayed. He Himself is the Lord our God; just as surely as He was with Joshua, so surely can we count upon Him to be with us whithersoever we go. If you and I will really believe this ninth verse of the first chapter of Joshua, we shall be able to face anything for our Lord.

NOVEMBER 21

Then Joshua commanded the officers of the people
(Josh. 1:10).

We were thinking yesterday of God's command to Joshua.
Can anyone doubt that Joshua obeyed that command? Not
in the light of the Scripture record of the victories at Jericho,
Ai, and Beth-horon can that be doubted.

And now we find Joshua commanding others. Having himself learned to obey orders, he is ready to issue orders to the
officers of the people. So the price of leadership is always
the ability to accept discipline. The one central requirement
of spiritual leadership is therefore submission to God. If you
and I would be of blessing to others, we must first of all
know what it means to obey the Lord's commands. God commanded Joshua; Joshua obeyed; Joshua commanded the officers of the people. That is the logical prerequisite of spiritual
leadership.

NOVEMBER 22

*Many, O Lord my God, are Thy wonderful works which
Thou hast done, and Thy thoughts which are to us-ward: they
cannot be reckoned up in order unto Thee: if I would declare
and speak of them, they are more than can be numbered* (Ps.
40: 5).

Verse three of this wonderful Psalm speaks of the new song
which God puts into the mouth of His redeemed and tells us
that its theme is praise. But may it not be that this fifth
verse gives us one way in which that song may be expressed?
For praise is a great theme, as vast as the wonderful works
of God. If we are to sing that song we must have words.
Now it is significant, going back once more to the third verse,
to note that God has put the new song in our mouths. Surely
this might well mean that we are to find in Scripture, which
is His Word, the actual words of our new song. All Christians
who love God's Word know the blessing of having it in their
hearts and upon their lips. Therefore from the spiritual point
of view, what more practical use could we make of ten or
fifteen minutes of our time set apart for God today than to
commit to memory the lovely setting forth of the new song
of praise found in this verse!

NOVEMBER 23

He hath committed all that he hath to my hand (Gen. 39:8).

We may find a two-fold message here as we think of Joseph, first as a type of Christ, and next as a type of the believer. As a type of Christ, he stands for the Lord Jesus into Whose pierced hand God has committed all things. But it is also true that to us there is given a similar responsibility. Our Lord has ascended. And He has left us with all of His glorious Gospel. Into our hands He has committed not only the one message of redemption for a lost world, but also His own good Name. For when we sin, our sin reflects upon the Lord Jesus Whose we are and Whose Name we bear. What an incentive to holy living! What a deterrent from submitting to temptation!

NOVEMBER 24

God is a Spirit; and they that worship Him must worship Him in spirit and in truth (John 4:24).

Religious liberty is one of our most cherished democratic principles; we insist that no man has the right to dictate how any other man should worship God. But there is a limit to religious liberty. The universe is a monarchy, not a democracy. He Who sits upon its throne is the Sovereign, and He has the eternal right to dictate how men are to worship Him. To be sure, the Sovereign God allows liberty in externals of worship, but when it comes to the heart of the matter, we find that the word "must" in His Son's teaching about worship invalidates the worship of millions today. And they are not all living in heathen lands; throughout Christendom there are many who are failing in the one essential of worshiping a Spiritual God in spirit and in truth. It is even possible for us Christians thus to fail. We have just to let our minds wander in prayer, we have only to go to church for outward show and not inward reverence, we have simply to let pride contaminate our religious activities, and we too may invalidate our worship.

NOVEMBER 25

My cup runneth over (Ps. 23: 5).

Let us make a sweeping comment upon that familiar word. There is not a Christian living, anywhere in the world, who ought not every day to make that sentence his own. For Christians have Christ, and Christ is All and in all. No sickness, no sorrow, no calamity, nothing can for a moment compare with the abundance of the blessings that are in Christ Jesus. Granted that outward circumstances may reach the extreme of distress, yet the unseen and therefore the real blessings of companionship with Christ are still overflowing. If you doubt this, delve into the biographies of the great missionary saints, the martyrs, and the heroes of the faith. "My cup runneth over" is always true of the soul who truly walks with the Lord Jesus Christ.

NOVEMBER 26

Be not afraid of their faces: for I am with thee to deliver thee, saith the Lord (Jer. 1:8).

"Afraid of their faces"! Is not that the root of much moral cowardice? We hesitate to speak the word of testimony, to rebuke flagrant evil, to side with the right, because we are afraid—not of men's blows, but of their faces. We fear the scornful look and the disdainful eye. Yes, if we are honest with ourselves, we must admit that we are naturally so weak as to be terrified by mere looks.

But, thank God, that is not all. For it was none other than the Almighty Who spoke these words to Jeremiah on the occasion of his call to prophesy. He knew that, like all men, Jeremiah might wilt under scorn. And so He gave the promise that drives out all fear, including the fear of men's faces. "I am with thee," He said. "I am with thee for a definite purpose—'to deliver thee'."

Christian believer, the same God Who called Jeremiah, assuredly calls you. There is someone to whom He would have you and you alone witness. There is some work for Him which only you can do. Rely therefore upon the invigorating word spoken not only to Jeremiah but also to you: "Be not afraid of their faces: for I am with thee to deliver thee."

NOVEMBER 27

Be glad in the Lord (Ps. 32: 11).

Let us think today regarding the nature of joy. Rejoicing is not an abstract matter; joy is always related to some object, person or thing. So we rejoice in our successes, our good fortune, our work, our health, and, if we rise to a higher level, in the successes and good fortune of others. In this kind of joy the world can and does participate. But there is another rejoicing that is distinctively Christian. There is the joy which David expresses in our text, "Be glad in the Lord." Other joys are transitory; this is permanent. Other joys depend upon circumstances and things; Christian joy depends upon the Lord. But it does not preclude any legitimate forms of gladness. Rather is it the basis for them, so that believers may rejoice in everything and in every proper relationship *in* their Lord.

NOVEMBER 28

And Manoah said, . . . How shall we order the child, and how shall we do unto him? (Judges 13:12).

The divine record makes clear the fact that Manoah and his wife, the parents of Samson, were a couple yielded to God. Humbly and prayerfully they received the angelic message regarding the son to be given them. And there is every reason to believe that they brought the child up in strict accord with divine counsel. Yet Samson went far astray. So has it always been. Godliness is not inherited. Environment and spiritual influences in the early years are vital, but in themselves they do not save a man. The decision to prefer Christ and His righteousness to the world is an intensely individual matter. Negatively made, it may nullify all the blessing of a godly home. Positively made, it may cancel even the darkest background. Rahab the harlot came out of a dreadful environment, yet her name lingers even today in the sacred genealogy of Christ. Samson, the son of God-fearing parents, perished a blinded slave in Philistia. Is your life stamped irrevocably with your very own decision for Christ and His righteousness?

NOVEMBER 29

The Word of the Lord which came unto Zephaniah . . .
(Zeph. 1:1)

What an audacious beginning! While the Dantes, Shakespeares and Miltons—the men of supreme genius—have not dared to use it, we find the obscure Zephaniah, Haggai, Zechariah, Micah, Jonah and many another boldly penning it. How thoughtlessly we read these familiar Old Testament phrases, "The word of the Lord came unto me," "The Lord spake," etc., without pausing to reflect upon their stupendous meaning. Almighty God, the Creator and Upholder of the Universe, expressing Himself through an insignificant Hebrew in an insignificant land long ago! Were we to realize more fully the miracle of inspiration, you and I should be more ready to give the greater heed to the Word of God.

NOVEMBER 30

Esther did the commandment of Mordecai, like as when she was brought up with him (Esther 2:20).

Let this be a word to parents, guardians, pastors, teachers—to all who have to do with youth. The fate of the most important nation in the world, God's chosen people, was hanging on the action of a comely young woman. And her course in this time of crisis depended upon her early training. Esther had evidently been committed to Mordecai, her elder cousin, for her upbringing. The emergency came, Israel was menaced by the mad hatred of Haman. But God is Sovereign. He knew in advance all the fury of the Jew-hater. Years before, He had been training a little girl under a faithful guardian. The storm broke, but the nation was saved through Esther. She had indeed "come to the kingdom for such a time as this."

Are you ever discouraged at the weariness that comes over all who are responsible for the training of youth? Then remember that a Christian child *does* follow the way in which he has been trained, granted that the training has been done in God's power. Who knows what great things God may do through some little one entrusted to your care?

DECEMBER 1

And the child Samuel grew before the Lord (I Sam. 2:21).

You do not have to be a child in years to take to yourself a lesson from this verse. Before you is a new month. How are you to grow during it? Of this you may be sure: your growth is before the Lord. He sees your development; old or young, you are growing in His sight. And that growth of yours is either in godliness or in worldliness. Souls do not stand still; they develop, and they develop according to the food they receive. Therefore, if you would grow in grace this month, feed your soul with the sincere milk of the Word and eat the Bread which came down from Heaven (John 6: 57, 58).

DECEMBER 2

Fear not; ye have done all this wickedness: yet turn not aside from following the Lord, but serve the Lord with all your heart (I Sam. 12:20).

One of the paralyzing consequences of sin is that it makes us say, "What's the use?" thus tempting us to abandon the struggle for righteousness. How openly and adequately Samuel met that difficulty for God's people! They had indeed sinned in that they, the very chosen people of Jehovah, had preferred to be ruled by a human king like the heathen instead of by God Himself. Yet, Samuel tells them, "Fear not. You have," he says, "indeed done wickedly; yet," he urges them, "follow on after the Lord despite your sin."

The principle is this. There are times when the best thing we can do is to consider the past a closed book. Did Israel reject their divine King? So have we; every time we have preferred sin to His will we have rejected His Sovereignty over us. Such things are irrevocable. And to let them alienate us further from a gracious Lord Who has forgiven them through the blood of His Son is simply to play into the devil's hands. Confess the sin. Then "Fear not . . . turn not aside from following the Lord, but serve the Lord with all your heart." That is God's will for His erring people.

DECEMBER 3

Doing the will of God from the heart (Eph. 6: 6).

These words occur in Paul's exhortation to servants who profess Christ. A glance at the Greek text shows us a significant thing. This is the single place in the whole New Testament where the word *psuche* is translated "heart." In every other of its many, many occurrences it is rendered "soul" or "life." It would seem, therefore, that there is no valid reason why it should not in this case read "soul," making the phrase, "doing the will of God from the *soul*." Thus rendered the exhortation strikes deeper than before. For, while the heart is the seat of the affections, the soul or *psuche* is the very center of the life. To do the will of God, therefore, is never a superficial thing; it goes right to the innermost springs of our beings. Right service for God means God-control extending right down into the soul.

DECEMBER 4

Then certain of the scribes answering said, Master, Thou hast well said. And after that they durst not ask Him any question at all (Luke 20: 39, 40).

Christ had proved His wisdom to the Pharisees, Sadducees and Scribes. Their attempts to catch Him by subtle questions had miserably wilted under His penetrating intellect. And so they brought Him this grudging compliment, "Master, Thou hast well said." Because of His wisdom, which pierced through their deceit, they dared not ask Him anything more.

How different is the truly Christian attitude toward the divine wisdom of the Lord Jesus! Believers find in Him, Who is wiser than Solomon, the answers to their most perplexing problems. They know that He has spoken well in the New Testament, and they also know that He has spoken well in hard places in their lives. For that very reason they do what His religious enemies were afraid to do—they ask Him questions. It is an inexpressible comfort to know that we may ask the Lord Jesus *anything*, that we may take *every* problem to Him.

DECEMBER 5

Then on that day David delivered first this psalm to thank the Lord into the hand of Asaph and his brethren (I Chron. 16:7).

Gratitude, one of the half-forgotten Christian virtues, was prominent in David's character. Established by God's help on the throne of Israel, he gave praise and thanksgiving to Him Whose sovereign grace had made him king. Analyze the prayer life of nine Christians out of ten and you will find a great dearth of thanksgiving. Sinners that we are, saved from a dreadful doom by the shed blood of God's only Son, sustained daily and hourly by divine mercy, blessed with many blessings, we all too seldom share the David attitude of thanksgiving. When is our prayer most fervent? When asking God for some new boon? When pleading for some fresh deliverance? Or when thanking Him for past blessing?

DECEMBER 6

And the house . . . was built of stone made ready before it was brought thither: so that there was neither hammer nor axe nor any tool of iron heard in the house, while it was in building (I Kings 6:7).

The silence with which those great stones were fitted into place is a parable. For "a greater than Solomon" is now engaged through His divine Administrator, the Holy Spirit, in building a greater temple. Peter tells us that it is made up of living stones. And this greater temple, even the church which is Christ's body, is also being erected silently. Why was Solomon's temple built quietly? Because each stone was perfectly fitted beforehand by the master workmen. So each living stone, each Christian life, is softly being prepared by the Holy Spirit for the living temple whose Cornerstone is the Lord Jesus.

God's work in this age does not necessarily proceed with clamor and outward show. We yearn for dramatic evidences of outward power, when all the time the Holy Spirit is secretly fashioning the living stones. Christian worker, are you willing to let God work in His own quiet way, even if by outward results men count you a failure?

DECEMBER 7

For the things which are seen are temporal; but the things which are not seen are eternal (II Cor. 4:18).

If only we Christians would remember this, we should be delivered from a vast amount of useless worry and concern. For the deep realization of this truth in any life leads to a radical transfer of inner residence. He who knows that only the unseen, spiritual things abide follows Paul's great imperative, "Set your affection on things above, not on things on the earth, for ye are dead, and your life is hid with Christ in God." There is a sense in which it is positively disgraceful for a believer in the Lord Jesus to be engrossed in purely material affairs. The Christian cannot withdraw from the world, but he can set his affection above the world in heavenly places with Christ.

DECEMBER 8

No man should be moved by these afflictions (I Thess. 3:3).

What does affliction do to you? Perhaps you are not yet able to answer that question because of lack of experience. Nevertheless, the day will come when you will be qualified to answer it, for none of us escapes trouble. Now Paul here implies that the important thing in affliction is not to be moved, which is another way of saying that the important thing is to preserve your balance and stand your ground. For your Christian life rests upon the unchanging love of the Heavenly Father. The storm may become a very hurricane, but it can never blow hard enough to move "the soul that on Jesus hath leaned for repose," especially when that soul realizes, as the rest of our verse puts it, "that we are appointed thereunto" (i.e., unto affliction). While God may not send directly every one of our troubles, yet He has appointed us to meet them. And the realization of the fact that not a single affliction is foreign to His loving interest or beyond His tender care stabilizes our wavering souls as nothing else can.

DECEMBER 9

And this is love, that we walk after His commandments
(II John, vs. 6).

The Word of God is very direct and simple regarding the
great principles of the spiritual life. It makes crystal clear,
for instance, what love entails. Over and over again, as in
this verse, it is made plain that the love of God must be
made manifest in an obedient walk. And so we must admit
that our spiritual failures never result from the obscurity
of God's Word, but from our unwillingness to do exactly
what that Word says. The church today needs more Christians
who are fundamentalists in obeying the Bible they so zeal-
ously defend.

DECEMBER 10

In My Father's house are many mansions (John 14: 2).

If we think for a moment about two words in this well
loved sentence, we shall see one of its most blessed shades
of meaning. They are "house" and "mansions," the first
being the very common Greek word, *oikos*, the second being
mone. *Oikos* is the regular Greek word for "house" or
"home," and is used very many times in the New Testament.
But *mone* is a much less common word, meaning an "abode"
or "dwelling place" and not a separate, self-contained residence as *oikos* implies.

Now this distinction is an important one. There is one
great heavenly home, which is the Father's house. In that
house or home there are many separate, individual abodes
or dwelling places. Godet's comment is enlightening: "The
image," he says, "is derived from those immense oriental
palaces in which there is an apartment, not only for the
sovereign and heir to the throne, but for all the king's sons,
however numerous they may be." The Lord Jesus, therefore,
is not talking about separate mansions, some larger and some
smaller than others. He is portraying a great family home,
presided over by the Eternal Father and having abundant ac-
commodations for every single child of God who has ever
lived or who ever will live.

DECEMBER 11

As much as in me is, I am ready to preach the Gospel (Rom. 1:15).

What an example Paul sets before us in this verse! "As much as in me is" means that with all his capacity, with every one of his consecrated faculties at work, he was ready to preach the Gospel to those in Rome. Without this qualification for effective witness, other things are relatively minor. Gifts of eloquence, intellect and personality, great learning and even piety can never be fully effective for God without the utter consecration implied in this simple phrase "as much as in me is." Think what blessing would come to many today if every Christian reading these words would really witness for Christ "as much as in (him) is"—just for this one day.

DECEMBER 12

God also hath . . . given Him a Name which is above every name (Phil. 2:9).

The Name of Jesus! Surely it is the touchstone between believer and unbeliever. The world still takes it in vain, perhaps never more freely than today. Yet for the Christian there is no other name that can compare with it. Cold of heart is the believer who is not cut to the quick when it is bandied about in profane talk.

But have you ever thought, dear friend, of what you may do to that Name which God has set above every name? You are a Christian, and therefore you bear the Name with you daily. You would rather have your tongue seared with fire than to use the Name of Jesus profanely. Ah, but when you relay that bit of idle gossip, when you give your friend that unkind word, when you engage in that doubtful business practice, or when temper or discouragement master you—what are you doing to the Name of Jesus? There are two forms of profane use of the Name—one by word, the other by deed.

DECEMBER 13

And ye shall seek Me, and find Me, when ye shall search for Me with all your heart (Jer. 29:13).

"With *all* your heart." That phrase explains why so many men and women do not find God. They do not find Him because they are seeking Him with divided hearts. Wholeheartedness is essential to any successful search, whether it be for gold or for God. And wholeheartedness in seeking God grows out of realization of need for Him. No sinner can ever find the Lord until he realizes his lost condition and his need of salvation.

Is not the trouble with many of us Christians simply the fact that we are not seeking God daily? Yes, He has found us in redemption through Christ. But, resting on past experiences, our hearts are divided between allegiance to God and allegiance to the world. Shall we not today wholeheartedly seek to know our Lord better?

DECEMBER 14

O Lord, my strength, and my fortress, and my refuge in the day of affliction (Jer. 16:19).

The appeal of these words is universal, because their message is so completely personal. They came straight from the heart of Jeremiah, a prophet whose life was one long round of misunderstanding and persecution. In every difficult day, Jeremiah's words go to the center of our need. They have supreme value, because they express so simply that which made Jeremiah's life such a marvel of fidelity to God. For him God was not only the Lord but *his* Lord; when Jeremiah called the Lord "*my* strength, and *my* fortress, and *my* refuge in the day of affliction," each repetition of the pronoun was like a hand gripping the Almightiness of God.

The most important thing about any man's knowledge of God is the extent to which it is personal. When it comes to the hard and perplexing and staggering things of life, only those who can say with Jeremiah, "O Lord, *my* strength, and *my* fortress, and *my* refuge," are able to know God's all-sufficiency.

DECEMBER 15

*And whiles I was speaking, and praying, and confessing my
sin and the sin of my people. . . . Yea, whiles I was speaking
in prayer, even the man Gabriel . . . touched me . . .* (Dan.
9: 20, 21).

Perhaps the most instructive of Old Testament saints, so
far as the prayer life goes, was Daniel. Here he received an
answer *while* he was praying. But notice how he was praying.
"Confessing my sin and the sin of my people." There we
have one of the missing elements of prayer today. No man
in the Bible had a more blameless record than Daniel, yet
personal confession stands in the very forefront of his great
and successful intercessory prayer.

DECEMBER 16

The very God of peace sanctify you wholly (I Thess. 5:23).

Is it not too bad that so many of us Christians are satisfied
with a comparatively low standard of spiritual life? In con-
tented resignation we accept only a portion of the blessing
and victory that God has for us. Yet all the time God desires
to give us His best.

Our verse for today makes this clear. "The very God of peace
sanctify you wholly," wrote Paul. He was not expressing an
impossibility when he sent those words to the Thessalonians.
There is a difference between eradication of the old nature,
which is an impossibility in this life, and sanctification. While
recognizing the incurable depravity of the carnal nature, Paul
more than once stressed the fact that God would have us depart
from all iniquity and that He would sanctify us wholly.

Why, then, should we be satisfied with anything less than
God's best? Indeed, such contentment with an inferior Christian life and experience is supremely dangerous, for it cannot
but mean resignation to some sin in our lives. And when we
become resigned to sin, sin has a way of growing in its grip
and power upon us.

May God make us believers discontented with anything less
than the highest life Christ has for us! God preserve us from
self-satisfied discipleship!

DECEMBER 17

Speak Lord; for Thy servant heareth (I Sam. 3:9).

When you and I are before the Lord in prayer, our attitude should be the one expressed by these words. To be sure, it may not be God's will to speak to us each time we pray. Yet there is always the possibility that He may speak, and there is the certainty that at times He does speak to His children. The important thing for us is to be receptive. God does not speak to closed ears. And when He does speak, He may not always say what we should like to hear. Yet hear Him we must, if we would remain in fellowship with Him and do His will.

Let this be our cry as we pray for guidance for this day's work: "Speak, Lord; for Thy servant heareth."

DECEMBER 18

Verily, verily, I say unto you, Ye seek Me, not because ye saw the miracle, but because ye did eat of the loaves, and were filled (John 6:26).

So it is possible to see a miracle and yet not see it. It is possible even to partake of the fruits of a miracle and be utterly blind to what has caused them. These people to whom the Lord Jesus was speaking had witnessed with their own eyes His multiplication of the loaves and fishes. Yet He had to say to them that they had never really seen the miracle. Why was this so? "Because," said the Lord Jesus, "ye did eat of the loaves and were filled." In other words, they were preoccupied with the material result of His power to such an extent that they overlooked its spiritual source.

Is it not true that many of us Christians are like these Galileans? We know from experience what Christ can do for us, and our attention gets focused upon what He can do to the extent that we forget the greater miracle, which is Himself. When we begin to love our Lord for Himself instead of for what He can give us; when we seek to have fellowship with Him just to be with Him, not merely to receive His gifts, then we are really growing in the knowledge of Christ.

DECEMBER 19

And Miriam and Aaron spake against Moses . . . And they said, Hath the Lord indeed spoken only by Moses? hath He not spoken also by us? And the Lord heard it (Num. 12: 1, 2).

"And the Lord heard it." Tragic words! Miriam and Aaron were doing what countless Christians have done. They were gossiping against their spiritual leader. Did you ever notice that the seed of their sin was pride? "Moses," they reasoned, "is not so great. He has not an exclusive access to God. God speaks also through us." Oh, it was all very plausible. "And the Lord heard it."

Take a few minutes to read the sequel to the story in the remainder of the chapter. Your heart will be searched and you will be humbled.

DECEMBER 20

And one of the malefactors which were hanged railed on Him, saying, If Thou be Christ, save Thyself and us (Luke 23:39).

Did you ever notice that the two thieves who were crucified alongside of Christ both had something to say to Him? But one was saved and the other lost. Why? The answer is very simple. These men spoke to the dying Saviour and their words revealed the attitude of their hearts toward Him.

Now it is perfectly true that the thief who was lost addressed the Lord as Christ. But he made a fatal mistake. He made the mistake of prefacing that Name with a little word of two letters—"if." "If," he said, "Thou be Christ." "If"—. And so that man was lost. For it is solemn truth that no man or woman or child will ever enter Heaven with a doubt in his heart regarding the Saviourhood of the Lord Jesus. Oh, they may not understand all about Him, but they must be sure that He is the Saviour of the world and their Saviour too.

Are you today sure that *your* sins are forgiven through the blood of Christ shed upon Calvary? Then are you living a life that will lead those about you who doubt His saving power to know Him as their divine Redeemer?

DECEMBER 21

That the Name of our Lord Jesus Christ may be glorified in you (II Thess. 1:12).

Paul's prayers for the various churches are notable for loftiness. He might have asked for their material prosperity. He might have prayed for a hundred and one lesser blessings. But the apostle had a great sense of proportion in prayer. And so, over and over again, we find him asking for the very highest for the churches committed to his care.

Our verse for today is a case in point. "That the Name of our Lord Jesus Christ may be glorified in you." Would you be willing to let all the smaller petitions go and ask God for just one thing—that Christ might be glorified in you? Well, if you are willing, you will find that the answer to that prayer carries with it the other necessary blessings.

DECEMBER 22

There remaineth yet very much land to be possessed (Josh. 13: 1).

Apply this word to yourself and see if it holds true of your life. How much of you does the Holy Spirit have? As you look at your life, must you say of yourself, "There remaineth yet very much of me to be possessed by the Spirit of Christ"?

Not until you have given God control of your whole body, all of your abilities, all of your business or profession, all of your recreations, all of your heart and mind and soul, all of yourself—not until then have you entered fully into what Christ has for you. And if there yet remains anything in you to be possessed by Christ, will you not today go before Him in prayer and ask Him to enter into some place or something in you from which He has hitherto been excluded? To make a daily habit of turning over to your Lord the unoccupied fields of your heart brings the unspeakable joy of the more abundant life.

DECEMBER 23

He is the Rock, His work is perfect. for all His ways are judgment: a God of truth and without iniquity, just and right is He (Deut. 32:4).

What a God those words from the song of Moses reveal! And yet there are some who persist in talking about "the primitive conceptions of God" the Israelites had. Away with all these notions of a "tribal Deity." The truth lies quite elsewhere. From the very beginnings of Scripture we find a God of infinite greatness. It is not for men today to criticize the God of the Old Testament. As Moses said, "He is a Rock, His ways are perfect." It is rather for men to come to Him by way of the Rock of Ages. Beware, O Christian, of becoming infected with the modern superficiality in thinking about Almighty God. He is not just a great, impersonal force, resident in some distant part of the universe. He is the "Rock . . . perfect . . . a God of truth . . . without iniquity, just and right."

DECEMBER 24

And it came to pass in those days, that there went out a decree from Caesar Augustus, that all the world should be taxed (Luke 2:1).

The great Roman Emperor, Caesar Augustus himself, issues a decree regarding taxation. In an obscure little province of the world-wide empire, a young man and his wife go to their native hamlet for the taxing, and a Babe is born. Caesar Augustus neither knew nor cared. But over seven hundred years before, the prophet Micah had pre-written the place of that humble birth (Micah 5:2). "God works in a mysterious way His wonders to perform; He plants His footsteps in the sea and rides upon the storm." And He also bends the world ruler to do His will. Tonight men and women the world over are thinking of the Babe of Bethlehem, while proud Caesar Augustus' memory is a thing of the dead past.

DECEMBER 25

She brought forth her firstborn Son . . . and laid Him in a manger (Luke 2:7)

He was a tiny Babe when He touched that manger. But His touch transformed it. And now, nineteen hundred years later, we are thinking of the manger with a peculiar sense of reverence. The infant Jesus touched it, and His touch transformed it into something of sacred meaning. So He Who was born in the stable transforms by a touch.

No Christian truth is merely abstract, least of all the truth of Christ's transforming power. Either He has touched your life and changed it or He has not touched it. Being a Christian means personal contact with the Saviour Who was born in Bethlehem. You say that you have had that saving contact with Him? Then make this joyful Christmas season the occasion to put someone else in touch with your transforming Lord.

DECEMBER 26

The Lord Himself shall give you a sign; Behold, a virgin shall conceive, and bear a Son, and shall call His Name Immanuel (Isa. 7:14).

This is the traditional season for remembering the birth of One Who came into the world long ago. And there is probably no single statement that more clearly demonstrates the uniqueness of that birth than this verse. The world venerates the anniversaries of the greatest of the past. But there is no other whose birth can be recalled with a statement written *over seven hundreds of years in advance of the event.* Yes, our verse for today is often quoted, but it is none the less a miracle. Every time it appears on a Christmas card it witnesses to the supernatural birth of the Babe of Bethlehem.

"Immanuel"! His divinely pre-written Name gives His divinely appointed message, "Immanuel—God with us." How sad that from the very beginning men had no room for Immanuel. How tragic that today there is still no room for Him. Room for war, room for sin, room for pleasure and lust —but no room for Immanuel. Oh, let our Christmas prayer be for men everywhere to open their hearts to Immanuel!

DECEMBER 27

And God is able to make all grace abound toward you; that ye, always having all sufficiency in all things, may abound to every good work (II Cor. 9:8).

Here we have the guarantee of victory over every difficulty. Following the eternal foundation of "God is able," there come these repeated and marvelously inclusive assurances— *"all grace—always—all sufficiency—all things—every good work."* You may take it on the Word of God Who cannot lie that there is no emergency, no sorrow, no problem, no calamity beyond the reach of His perfect grace. Today or tomorrow your need may assume in your troubled eyes stupendous proportions. Have no fear. You have the assurance of "always having all sufficiency in all things."

Finally, why is this glorious promise given to us? Simply, as Paul tells us, that we "may abound to every good work."

DECEMBER 28

Thou hast kept the good wine until now (John 2:10).

In saying this the ruler of the marriage feast at Cana expressed the way in which Christ deals with His own. As Dr. J. Stuart Holden pointed out in speaking of this verse, the devil gives his servants the best first. Then, after having lured them with the pleasures of the world, he pays them their wages of death. But Christ treats His servants differently. As time passes He gives them more and more blessing, so that those who have served Him longest and know Him most intimately exclaim, "Thou hast kept the best blessing until now." A well-loved chorus puts it, "Every day with Jesus is sweeter than the day before;" but the apostle expresses it best of all when he writes, "Eye hath not seen, nor ear heard, neither have entered into the heart of man, the things which God hath prepared for them that love Him" (I Cor. 2:9). Yes, Christ keeps the best until the last, and no tongue can tell the boundless blessings He has for His own.

DECEMBER 29

And the name of the city from that day `shall be, The Lord is there (Ezek. 48:35).

Thus Ezekiel's great prophecy ends. In the last chapters of the book he has been describing the glory of the millennial temple and the New Jerusalem. Detail after detail is given regarding the temple and the land. But the prophetic picture ends with this finely reticent note, "The Lord is there." No pen can describe Him, no tongue can do justice to His glory. The highest thing that can be said is this simple statement, "The Lord is there." That is the ultimate glory, that is Heaven itself, the place where the Lord abides in all the beauty of holiness. Oh, how thankful we Christians should be to the Redeemer Who has with His precious blood purchased our way into that city whose name for all eternity is, "The Lord is there."

DECEMBER 30

Grow in grace, and in the knowledge of our Lord and Saviour Jesus Christ (II Peter 3:18).

An exhortation such as this has not only a forward but also a backward look. And because this is the close of the year, let us take it today in a retrospective sense. Let us just ask ourselves some questions in the privacy of our hearts and before God alone: "Have I during the past twelve months really grown in grace? Do I have a fuller knowledge of my Lord and Saviour Jesus Christ than I had last January? Has the year meant for me spiritual progress or has it meant retrogression?" May God help us honestly to face these questions!

And if we can truly say to our Lord Jesus that we know Him better than a year ago and that we have truly grown in His grace, let us give Him *all* the praise. But if we must with downcast eyes confess to spiritual retrogression, may Christ Himself help us here and now to make that complete surrender which always spells growth in grace and in the glorious knowledge of Him.

DECEMBER 31

Great is Thy faithfulness (Lam. 3:23).

Not a single Christian who reads these four words but does not have cause to utter them today out of a thankful heart. For another year is at its end. And through it all God has again proved Himself faithful. "But," someone may say, "my blessings have not been so many this year as before." And another may add, "But there has been so much trial in my life during the past twelve months." Yes, for some of us these things are true. They were certainly true for Jeremiah, who wrote the words of our text, for if ever a book came out of affliction, Lamentations did. Yet we can still say with grateful hearts, "Great is Thy faithfulness." For if blessings have been meager, there is the possibility that we have been limiting God by refusing to rely upon His promises, and, in the exercise of real faith, to take Him at His Word. Or it may be that our heavenly Father in His faithful love for our souls has been letting us go through fiery trial for our discipline and the forging of a stronger hold upon Him. It still remains that with Him there is "no variableness, neither shadow of turning." Let us, therefore, bless the Lord in our souls and cry out to Him Who loves to the end, "Great is Thy faithfulness."

FOR SPECIAL TIMES

GOOD FRIDAY

And I, if I be lifted up from the earth, will draw all men unto Me (John 12:32).

Nineteen centuries have not changed an iota the truth of those words of Christ. The Cross is still God's only way of attracting men. On no other basis does He draw them to Himself. The Cross is universally efficacious. It draws poor as well as rich, ignorant as well as learned, savage as well as civilized. It has drawn you as well as me, just as it will draw every man, woman, or child who ever will be saved in the future. Oh, for more ministers who are not ashamed to place the Cross foremost in their preaching! *Their* sermons will not lack drawing power. Oh, for more laymen who are willing to testify to the power of the Cross in their lives! *They* will win souls. Christ has promised that when He is lifted up from the earth, He will draw all men unto Him. How dare we lift up anyone or anything aside from Him?

When Jesus therefore had received the vinegar, He said, It is finished: and He bowed His head, and gave up the ghost (John 19:30).

Before this sacred scene we can only bow in awe and adoration. His work was done. He "Who knew no sin" had been made sin for us. He had borne "our sins in His own body on the tree." And, having power to lay down His life and to take it again, He voluntarily laid it down. These words, "It is finished," were, as the other Gospels imply, uttered as a triumphant shout. They were a cry of victory, and as such they echo through the ages. They stand for the essence of our most holy faith, to be guarded against all systems of error that would deny the completeness of Christ's atonement. Let us praise God that in Christ salvation is *fully* efficacious. He Who cried "It is finished" is sufficient for our *every* need.

EASTER

They found the stone rolled away (Luke 24:2).

Let us not forget that the Easter message is a message based on historical reality. There was an actual stone rolled against the door of a real tomb. That stone was truly removed, that tomb was indeed empty; the physical body it had contained was gone, later to be seen again as a glorified but real body, bearing the print of the nails and the mark of the spear. Deny these facts and you strike at the foundations of the faith. "If Christ be not raised," said Paul "your faith is vain, ye are yet in your sins." Whatever skepticism may say, the fact remains that on the first Easter day the tomb was empty, and the Christ Who showed Himself alive to His followers had actually arisen from the dead. Are you this Easter Day rejoicing in Him as the Lord Whose resurrection power gives you joy and peace and victory over sin?

Whom God hath raised up, having loosed the pains of death: because it was not possible that He should be holden of it (Acts 2:24).

These words from Peter's great Pentecost sermon emphasize the impossibility of our Lord's body remaining in the tomb. Just as surely as God kept His word about the prophesied burial of His Son, so He kept it as to His resurrection.

But even had there been no single prophecy of the resurrection, it would still have been bound to occur. And the reason is a very plain one. Christ *had* to rise from the dead because He was Christ. Man is man, a creature of the dust. But Christ is more than a man; He is God manifest in the flesh. And therefore the grave could not hold Him. For no grave is deep enough, no death is strong enough to hold God in thrall. It is a serious thing to deny the actual resurrection of the Lord Jesus, because to do so cannot but mean denial of His Deity. Believe that Christ never rose and you cannot believe that He is the divine Saviour.

Do you believe in the Deity of your Lord? Then rejoice today in the fact of His resurrection, and know that His power is available for you.

IN TIME OF TROUBLE

They came unto the iron gate . . . which opened to them of his own accord (Acts 12:10).

Peter's miraculous deliverance from prison is a great type of the way God deals with difficulties in the Christian life. When He is leading us, no barrier can stand. It is the universal experience of the saints that, when insurmountable difficulties have been faced, suddenly the way has been opened by God's power. How true it is that our part is but to follow on where God leads! There may be fast closed doors, double locked and barred against us. But if God is leading, the gates will open before us. Samuel Rutherford beautifully voiced this truth in his *Letters*. "What iron gates or bars," he wrote, "are able to stand it out against Christ? for when He bloweth, they open to Him."

Why are ye troubled? (Luke 24:38).

Well, *why* are you troubled? Because you have fallen into some sin? Then remember that "if we confess our sins, He is faithful and just to forgive us our sins, and to cleanse us from all unrighteousness." Because you are overwhelmed by weakness? Then hear Him Who says, "My grace is sufficient for thee; for My strength is made perfect in weakness." Because fear harasses you? Then know that "perfect love casteth out fear." Because you are weary? Then wait upon the Lord, knowing that they that do so "shall run and not be weary." Because you are sick? Then look to Him "Who healeth all (thy) diseases" and Who has promised to "make all thy bed in thy sickness." Because you are burdened with care? Then cast "all your care upon Him, for He careth for you." Because a great sorrow has come into your life? Then know that you have "the Comforter, that He may abide with you forever."

Above all, dear friend, know this. There is no human trouble whatever that is beyond your Saviour's ken; there is no difficulty He cannot perfectly, completely, and finally settle for you. "Earth hath no sorrows that Heaven cannot cure."

IN SICKNESS

Lord, behold, he whom Thou lovest is sick (John 11:3).

The words originally referred to Lazarus, but there is a sense in which they apply to everyone. For Christ loves the whole, lost world; He came to die for the sins of all. And He is interested in everyone. If you are lying ill as you read these words, then remember that it is *you* whom Christ loves. Or if your relative or friend is in sickness, remember that the words apply there also. Perhaps the illness has its spiritual as well as physical side. Still it remains true that he whom the Lord loves is sick.

When He heard therefore that he (Lazarus) was sick, He abode two days still in the same place where He was (John 11:6).

What must have been the thoughts of Mary and Martha as they waited for the beloved Physician and marked the dreary hours by watching their brother die! Surely the joy that had risen at the thought of Jesus' help waned with His unaccountable absence and died with their brother's death. Yet they had called for Jesus, and Jesus had heard their call. And then in a very few days He Who had so inscrutably delayed to answer the most urgent plea of His dearest friends demonstrated the divine wisdom of His delay. Had He come immediately, there would have been one more healing among many; by His tarrying Mary and Martha and the Jews and the whole world were reached by the mighty miracle of Lazarus' raising, and God was marvelously glorified.

Ah, yes, dear friend, your need may be desperate. Like Mary and Martha you may have called a Lord Who does not seem to come. How you need Him right now, in the midst of your distress! Yet He tarries. But be in peace. You have done the one essential thing; you have called the great Physician, and, though His apparent delay may seem disastrous, you may be absolutely certain that you will one day look upon the sequel and glorify Him. If you have called Jesus, He *will* help you and He will do it gloriously. But you must trust Him to work in His own time and in His own way.

BEREAVEMENT

And when the Lord saw her, He had compassion on her, and said unto her, Weep not (Luke 7:13).

The sentence comes from Luke's record of the healing of the son of the widow of Nain. The miracle is preeminent in its portrayal of the Lord's compassion. No one called upon Him to help, the stricken mother did not cry aloud for mercy; but the very pathos of that funeral procession spoke to His sympathetic heart with accents far louder than words. And, without being asked, purely out of the volition of His compassionate grace, He raised the widow's son. Thus always it is with our Lord and human sorrow. Our griefs are His; He knows our sorrows, and, as we suffer, His heart is indeed moved with compassion for us.

Precious in the sight of the Lord is the death of His saints (Ps. 116:15).

There are only a few things relating to Christians which God calls by the word "precious." One of them is their faith (II Peter 1:1); another, as in this verse and also in Psalm 72:14, is their death; and still a third is the redeeming blood of Christ. But why is the death of the Lord's saints so precious to Him Who has at His disposal the riches of the whole universe? First of all, we should understand who the saints are. Taking the term in its New Testament sense we recognize that it means all who have believed in the Lord Jesus Christ unto their soul's salvation. It is their death, not just the death of some preëminent model of piety, canonized by men, that is precious in the Lord's sight.

But why is the death of every saint, every godly person, young or old, weak or strong so valuable to the God of heaven and earth? Surely all of us who know the Gospel know the answer. The death of the saints is precious, because it is linked with the redemptive work of Christ. In the Person of His Son, God gave the most precious thing in all the universe to save us sinners. And when a saint (i. e., a saved sinner) dies, the redeeming purpose of God is consummated, as another soul goes to heaven, saved by the precious blood of Jesus.

INDEX